THE
ONLY
WAY TO
WIN

ALSO BY JIM LOEHR

Mental Toughness Training for Sports
Breathe In, Breathe Out
Toughness Training for Life
The New Toughness Training for Sports
Stress for Success
The Power of Full Engagement
The Power of Story

THE ONLY WAY TO WIN

How Building Character Helps
You Achieve More and Find Greater
Fulfillment in Business and Life

JIM LOEHR

HYPERION

NEW YORK

For my Father (Con) and Mother (Mary)
and for my three sons (Mike, Pat, and Jeff),
for being my greatest character teachers.

CONTENTS

PART IV: BACK TO CHASING ACHIEVEMENT
AGAIN—WITH THE NEW SCORECARD

When Socrates was unjustly imprisoned and facing imminent death, his jailers asked why he was not preparing for death. His response was simply "I've been preparing for death all my life by the life I've led."

—COACH JOHN WOODEN
IN *HOW TO BE LIKE COACH WOODEN* BY PAT WILLIAMS

AUTHOR'S NOTE

The names and identifying details concerning some individuals, as well as some elements of these individuals' stories, have been changed to protect their privacy.

THE
ONLY
WAY TO
WIN

INTRODUCTION

Scott sits four feet across from me, a look of pained recognition in his eyes, and he appears nauseated. His annual salary is somewhere north of a million dollars (not including bonus). He owns three homes, never flies commercial, and commands the faithful service, perhaps even respect, of twenty-four hundred employees. At this very minute, though, this CEO looks as if he is quite literally about to throw up. I wish I could tell you it's the first time I've witnessed such a moment.

"I've been blinded by my ambition," he says in a voice that is both biting and resigned. "Last night, when you had me examine my deepest values and examine how I've lived my life, it hit me like a freight train. I now realize that I've been hiding from the truth all along. I've been so eager to get to the top that I neglected the people and compromised the causes that meant the most to me. In a sense, I sold my soul. According to what I thought I wanted, I achieved it all. I'm pretty much on top of the world. But according to what I really feel matters to me—my family, my health, my relationships— I've failed. To be honest, I've known for a long time that at some level, what I was chasing was futile."

Then this man, this winner at all things, abruptly goes quiet— mystified, stunned, disillusioned.

Scott's profound realization occurred on Day 2 of a two-and-a-half-day workshop, one we've been conducting for fifteen years at the Human Performance Institute (HPI), a company I cofounded in 1992 with famed biomechanics researcher Jack Groppel. At HPI, we specialize in helping individuals and teams perform at the highest possible levels in high-stress environments. I've had many of these encounters with high achievers before, in both the world of sport, where I had the privilege of working with sixteen world number ones, and the world of business, where I counseled countless executives. All felt an irresistible need to confess that for years they had been chasing things that lack value. Seduced by a false promise of happiness, they devoted most of their energy to things that weren't very fulfilling. As a result, while they had successfully achieved most, if not all, of the key indices of success in our society—power, status, beauty, fame, money, and other material wealth—somehow, feelings of dissatisfaction and disillusionment persisted.

This book is not going to be a book about the evils of money, status, and other "superficial" markers of achievement. I will not suggest that you reject material things, creature comforts, luxury, a nice home, beautiful cars, or titles of prominence (whether that title be CEO or Wimbledon champion). Anyone familiar with my work over the years—virtually an entire career devoted to trying to help people accomplish great things—would find it quite incongruous for me to write a book explicitly assaulting the value of personal achievement.

The problem, as I've come to see it with ever-increasing clarity, is how the blind pursuit of external achievement can, even when successful, result in profound emptiness for all of us. Years of work with superstars, high achievers, and otherwise rich and famous clients have profoundly affected my understanding of achievement motivation and goal setting. I've witnessed that it is not just Scott the CEO millionaire who feels as I've described him feeling, not just the Olympic gold medalist who wonders "Is that all there is?" Nor is it only the C-suite executive, the partner at a big law firm, or the Ivy League graduate who feels dissatisfied despite the outward success.

It's also the salesperson, the middle manager, the nurse, or the stay-at-home mom or dad who often suffers a similar plight. Why is that? Because the system that stirs these feelings is one that we all helped to create—leaders, managers, coworkers, coaches, teachers, and parents. It's especially troubling that the roots of this system run so deep and wide that our children can't help but drink from the same well: They are being nurtured in such a way that many of them will suffer much the same lack of fulfillment that so many of their parents do.

In our work with thousands of clients, my colleagues and I have noted that it seems almost not to make a difference how much the individual earns or how apparently nice his or her home is. Does it really matter that Julie earns ten times what Earl earns, if the emptiness experienced by each is the same? What matters is the goals one has pursued—both the sacrifices one has made to achieve them and the obsessiveness (even addictiveness) with which one has pursued them—and the intrinsic satisfaction one has received from the pursuit.* And we have found that in most cases our clients are operating under assumptions about the personal return on their achievements that have not only failed to work but, astonishingly, have never even been properly vetted.

Ponder these if-then statements for their inherent promise:

If I summit Mount Everest, then I'll feel like I'm someone special.

If I win an Olympic medal, then I'll finally be happy with myself.

If I graduate from an Ivy League school, then it will give me the self-confidence I need to be successful in life.

If I finally get my medical degree, then it will all have been worth it.

If I get that next promotion, I'll finally feel like a success as a leader.

If I buy a home in my dream neighborhood, then I'll be someone.

If I finally get out from under all this financial pressure, then my happiness will improve significantly.

---

* The distinction between intrinsic and extrinsic motivation is an important one and will be explained in more detail in the chapters to follow. For now, suffice it to say that intrinsic motivation means engaging in an activity for the enjoyment of the activity itself, whereas extrinsic motivation means engaging in an activity for the desired end state, such as money.

If I write a best-selling book, then I'll be a success.

I'll be someone. I'll feel good about myself. I'll have value. I'll be a success.

We believe such positive feelings are achievable through external achievements like these because various promises have been made to us, relentlessly, from earliest memory. Achievement is viewed as the foundation for a successful life, for stable self-esteem, for fulfillment, and for living a life of significance and meaning.

All of that would be wonderful except for one thing.

These promises are all false.

Most of us have been adhering to measures of achievement that, when we really stop to think about them, don't matter to us. Or they matter to us disproportionately. A simple analysis would reveal that the benefit we get from the achievement by itself may not nearly be worth the energy and time we invest—or, as well-being experts Ed Diener and Robert Biswas-Diener memorably said about money, "Income appears to buy happiness, but the exchange rate isn't great."

If what matters most is not the actual winning or achievement in and of itself, then what *does* truly matter? It has something to do with the goals you choose, of course, because each goal has consequences. But to my mind, what truly matters most—and these are the questions I've obsessed over, studied, explored, and tried to articulate for the past three decades of my career and life—is this: Who do you become as a result of the pursuit of your goals? Who have you become as a consequence of the chase?

I WAS AS GUILTY AS anybody of chasing achievement. I defined myself by my job and the money I was making. Had someone asked me who I was without those things, I would have had no answer. As with the overwhelming majority of my clients, my life had been an achievement race to secure a sense of personal value. As with so many of them, much of my value became linked to external markers of success. *If I work with famous people, then I must be someone special. If the world's best athletes request my services, then I must be someone of value. If I build my own successful business, then I must be a success as a person.*

But the more I listened to my successful clients, the more I noticed something very odd: Their impressive achievements and the satisfaction reaped from them were usually not related. The chase itself had become obsessive, devoid of lasting enjoyment or fulfillment. Regardless of the size of the external win, the person's sense of satisfaction never changed much. This insight would have profound implications for me.

I learned that when achievement fails to deliver the anticipated satisfaction and fulfillment, it's typical to conclude that the fulfillment void was due to the fact that one simply didn't achieve enough. You need to push harder and achieve more—more money, more titles, more power, more tangible indices of success.

Tragically, the push to achieve can itself become an addiction, and like an addict, you're only as good as your last achievement fix. The result is protracted frustration and disillusionment.

"WHAT THE HELL IS wrong with me . . . I'm the number one tennis player on earth, and yet I feel empty . . . I've had the wrong goals." I literally came out of my chair when I read these words from Andre Agassi's startlingly frank and insightful autobiography, *Open*. The words were almost verbatim what we've heard from the countless high achievers in our programs. When I came upon Andre's confession, "I've been let in on a dirty little secret: winning changes nothing," my heart nearly jumped out of my chest. I'd found it! The tersest expression of the truth I'd been witnessing throughout my professional life: External achievement, in and of itself, will not and cannot fill the basic needs we have as human beings.

That Andre was the one to express these sentiments should not have surprised me. I was first introduced to him at the Nick Bollettieri Tennis Academy, when he was fourteen years old. I was responsible for the mental training of the two hundred plus players residing there. Of all the students, Andre was, hands down, my least favorite: suspicious, sarcastic, obstinate, distant, guarded, angry, rebellious. His personal style made him an exceptional challenge to teach. Was he gifted? Ridiculously so, with amazingly fast feet and hands and quick eyes. Everyone in tennis knew he had the raw physical talent to become a successful playing professional. Would he, though? That was a different matter. So many personal barriers stood between him and the realization of his vast potential. His childhood and adolescence were marked by deep, almost constant psychological pain. His father demanded things that made Andre constantly anxious and guilty. He felt psychologically off-balance always. Not in control. Unsafe.

At sixteen, Andre turned pro, eventually rising to number one in the world. He would forge one of the great careers in tennis history, winning eight Grand Slam singles titles (including the career Grand Slam) and an Olympic gold medal, as well as twice helping the U.S. to win the Davis Cup.

Given his astonishing accomplishments, if success breeds happiness, then Andre should have been the poster child for fulfillment. Sadly, the achievements hardly mattered at all to him. As his candid words convey, he gained no pleasure, no sense of fulfillment or peace from the majority of his celebrated tennis feats—even though he believed he should: "I try to talk myself out of [doom]. I tell myself that you can't be unhappy when you have money in the bank and own your own plane."

In 1997, at a point in his career when Andre was noted more for his unfulfilled promise than for his achievement, his world ranking slipped, then slipped some more, until he finally sank all the way to 141. He tried crystal meth and failed a drug test administered by the Association of Tennis Professionals. When the ATP alerted him to the positive test, he lied to them, claiming in a letter that he'd accidentally ingested a spiked drink at a party.

And then, at his lowest, Andre had the courage to reinvent himself. What made his reinvention special, what made it work for him, was jettisoning the "wrong goals" (as he wrote) and replacing them with new goals that would sustain him, regardless of whether he ever won another Grand Slam or tournament. He had been thinking about such a new goal for a while. "This is the only perfection there is, the perfection of helping others. This is the only thing we can do that has any lasting value or meaning. This is why we're here. To make each other feel safe." When he finally determined his own grand purpose in life and followed it, he had the persistence and focus to turn his life around. When he re-purposed his tennis to "help others feel safe," a transformation occurred. The game which he had always hated became a priceless gift. Now, while still ostensibly pursuing external achievements, he had established a completely different mind-set for doing so.

He could now leverage the fame and money from tennis to fulfill his grand purpose. What that meant for Andre was starting a charter school for disadvantaged kids. The distance Andre traveled from a troubled, confused, self-absorbed, fragile teenager to the man he has become, finally able to link tennis with his core purpose, is a remarkable journey, one I will document toward the end of the book. It's important to understand that Andre Agassi was not alone in this high-performance achievement trap. Nearly all of us, superstars or not, struggle at some level to resolve this agonizing personal crisis.

To better understand how the insights and recommendations contained in this book came to be, I need to give you a little historical perspective. Every year, more than two thousand high-achieving executives go through our multiday executive course. A significant component of the training is having each person create a document that describes as precisely as possible his or her life mission (we call it the Ultimate Mission in our training). We also ask our clients to write about their "best selves," when they are most proud of who they are. Analysis of both of these documents over many years has provided real insight into the value orientations of large numbers of executives. Perhaps most intriguing was our discovery that the things that executives most valued in themselves related to the way they inter-acted and connected with others. Issues of integrity, caring for oth-ers, trustworthiness, compassion, kindness, and humility invariably topped the list. Issues of fame, money, power, status, titles, material possessions, etc., rarely made the cut. Also interesting was our find-ing that virtually every Ultimate Mission crafted by the executives was about extending their sphere of influence. A successful life was contingent on how they connected and contributed to the lives of others. These responses led us directly to the doorstep of character.

This fundamental insight got us to rethink how achievement should be positioned in people's lives. Rather than an end in itself, it becomes a means to an end, a vehicle for building ethical strengths of character that do in fact produce enduring feelings of worthiness, fulfillment, and life satisfaction. For us at the Institute, all external achievements can become re-purposed to build character strengths that define success in the most important sense. By doing so, an en-tirely new scorecard takes form that defines winning in terms of the way one interacts with others. This is what is meant by ethical char-acter. When executives win with character, not only will they build a leadership legacy that lasts, they will experience enduring feelings of fulfillment and satisfaction.

THIS BOOK OFFERS A real solution to the achievement trap plagu-ing legions of people in today's high-stress, demanding world. This solution, which is both novel and research-based, takes the reader into the very heart of character development and links it to the world of achievement motivation in a way that produces stunning, immensely practical insights.

As our clients have discovered, something magical happens when the achievement of an extrinsic goal, like becoming VP or general manager, or hitting the twenty-year mark at your company, is rede-fined to become an opportunity to build specific strengths of charac-ter that reside at the epicenter of one's grand purpose for living. The addiction, emptiness, and chronic dissatisfaction begin to dissolve into longed-for feelings of worthiness, fulfillment, and well-being. And equally exciting has been our discovery that not only does one get a positive, enduring personal return for the energy invested in the pursuit of the achievement, but one actually starts performing at higher levels as well. Happier, more fulfilled people, I have learned, perform better under conditions of high stress than those who are not. It's clearly a win-win-win situation. Achieving with character is a win for you, a win for your employer, and a big win for the broader world in which you live.

There are many scorecards in life, and the first part of this book explores how society's scorecard has become the de facto scorecard for so many of us, why this happens, and why it leaves us feeling so empty. The second part of the book details how to create your own scorecard, with provocative exercises to get you going. The third part of the book applies character building to the worlds of business, sport, and parenting. The fourth part of the book explores the stories of several people who have gotten their story about achievement right, and how that has made all the difference.

Changing the scorecard, as this book will show, changes everything.

PART I

THE FALSE PROMISE OF ACHIEVEMENT

1

A Parade of Failed Promises

We are never deceived; we deceive ourselves.
—Goethe

et's get right to it. What are the failed promises that fuel the
achievement disillusionment? There are many but here are
four big ones:

Great achievements bring lasting happiness and fulfillment.
Great achievements lead to stable self-esteem.
Great achievements build strong character.
Great achievements define the foundation for a successful life.

To begin our understanding of how such promises are flawed,
let's start at the end.

Imagine a moment in the twilight of life. If you were casting a
backward glance, what might a life of true success, triumph, and
meaning look like? I'm continually astonished at how well people
answer this question, and more astonished still at how well many of
even the teenagers we've worked with respond to it. Putting aside
lame excuses and shallow reasoning, an accurate, though potentially
quite painful, assessment emerges. By doing this exercise, you can
start to determine if the investments you're making today and tomorrow give you the best chance of arriving at the end of your life
in a way you envisioned.

Go ahead. Take yourself to the end of your life. The truth, good or bad, is there.

Now come back to the present moment.

Get a pencil. Rank-order from 1 to 10 the values you most want your life to reflect. This is your vision, the most personal of visions.

_____wealth (the amount of money you have)

_____material possessions (how much stuff you've acquired)

_____family (however you define it)

_____social status (job titles, awards, trophies, certifications, degrees)

_____health (physical, mental, and emotional)

_____power (how many people you control)

_____ethical character (your expression toward others of love, kindness, honesty, generosity, gratitude, etc.)

_____fame (how many people know you)

_____attractiveness (the importance of looking good, beauty, etc.)

_____performance at work (your competence and mastery)

Now consider the time and energy you've invested over the last several years, and rank these values from 1 to 10 based on how much time and energy you've actually invested in each.

_____wealth

_____material possessions

_____family

_____social status

_____health

_____power

_____ethical character

_____fame

_____attractiveness

_____performance at work

Are the rankings on the two lists identical? Are they similar? Is there alignment between what you say is important in your life and your actual life?

On which of these items do you expend the most energy? Which items are you likelier to reference, consciously or not, to validate how you're doing in life?

If you died tomorrow, would you be okay with how you made out these lists, the extent to which they aligned, and what they say about how you lived your life?

Week after week, year after year, high achievers from nearly every walk of life—business, sport, medicine, military—come through one of our programs and confront the misalignment in their lives and are shocked at what they find. In one way or another, most people realize that they are not living the life they aspire to live.

WHILE REACHING THE TOP OF THE WORLD, I LOST MY NOSE AND MY FAMILY NEARLY LOST ME

Why does someone climb Mount Everest? To be able to say one has set foot on the highest point on earth? To push up against one's physical limits or extend them? To cross off another item on one's bucket list?

Does one attempt to summit Mount Everest to feel omnipotent? To feed an unquenchable thirst for achievement?

Or does one climb it, as it's often said with a shrug of the shoulders, simply because it's there?

I would suggest two very fundamental reasons many people attempt such feats:

- Visible achievements represent the most salient evidence that we were here on planet Earth. ("We are born with the powerful urge to have an effect on and master our environment," write A. J. Elliot, H. A. McGregor, and T. M. Thrash.)

- The acclaim, prestige, fame, wealth, power, and more that result from such achievements are markers that society values, and being valued in this way makes us feel good.

Texas pathologist Beck Weathers barely and famously survived the deadliest day in Mount Everest's history—May 11, 1996, when eight climbers died during summit attempts. Weathers lost his right hand, part of his right arm, all the fingers on his left hand, parts of both feet, and his nose, which was reconstructed with tissue from his ear and forehead. Here's his perspective on what's behind his, and many others', wish to climb Mount Everest, or complete any similar achievement conquest: "So much of our society is driven to succeed and to have that kind of single-minded focus that brings success. You think, from the business side, I'm doing it for my family, [but] it's a great rationalization, I've used it myself many times. But the fact is that's how you live life, that's your pattern of behavior, and it's very difficult to slow down long enough to examine that. . . . That's the part that rarely gets told." The pursuit of Everest, Weathers has said, was a "monkey on my back." To expel that monkey, was it okay for him to be absent from the people he supposedly cared about, to "force them to make a life for themselves"? Was getting the monkey off his back, or trying to, a worthwhile trade-off for his nose, several other body parts, and the "destroyed . . . relationships" with those who mattered to him?

I don't suggest that there is never a good reason to climb Mount Everest; there absolutely is. I am suggesting that the reason behind the pursuit should be examined far more closely. In the words of Weathers, "That's the part that rarely gets told." If people took a closer look, they would be shocked by what they found, would abandon the pursuit instantly, and replace it with the quest for something the motivation for which stands up to any level of scrutiny.

Similarly, why does one give so much time and energy to succeed at an incredibly demanding job? Why does one pursue fame? Why does one work extra hard all weekend for several years to save the money to buy one's dream house or spend endless hours watching one's child practice and compete at a sport? Why does one work so hard to get one's golf handicap under 10 or work nights and weekends for several years to earn an advanced degree?

As I said: There *are* good reasons to do these things. But we always need to ask ourselves why we're investing so much time and energy in the activities that consume most of our waking lives—questions like:

- When is the price of a goal attainment too high? What's the potential cost to you or others for the achievement?
- Is the sacrifice that goes into the pursuit justified in terms of what really matters?
- If, as a consequence of the pursuit, you pay an incredibly steep price, perhaps even the ultimate price—compromise your character, lose your family, lose your health, lose your life—will that be okay? Can you still justify going after that goal?
- When is the payoff not worth the price?
- How far will you go to achieve your goal?
- How much control do you have over realizing your achievement?
- Do you like who you are becoming as a consequence of the pursuit?
- Why are you seeking this achievement?
- What will happen to you and others if you fail?

"If you're going to pursue a dream, that's good—if it's a good dream," said Weathers after his life-changing catastrophe. "Simply getting excited about going into a place like Everest is not a sufficient reason to be there." Your dream may be intrinsically driven—to climb Mount Everest simply for the enjoyment of the adventure—but have you fully considered the potential consequences of the pursuit?

And consider something else: Are you pursuing a dream that *you chose* or one that society has *chosen for you*?

What matters aren't the markers that society values. "It's not the mountain we conquer, but ourselves," said Sir Edmund Hillary who, with Tenzing Norgay, became the first human to summit Everest. No one aspires to have descriptions etched onto their tombstones that speak to their extrinsic success. HERE LIES THE 30TH RICHEST MAN IN AMERICA . . . Is that really the epitaph one intends to leave behind?

What matters is that first list you rank-ordered a couple of pages ago. Where did wealth, power, social status, etc., rank when everything else was considered?

A TRAGIC TRADE-OFF

One thing that matters is being alive, healthy, and present.

Normally I would not write such an obvious sentence. Being any and all of those three things would seem the trademark of any "winner." But apparently it is not so obvious, if you go by the way so many people treat their physical selves. An alarming 40 percent of corporate executives are clinically obese. People never shut down from their exhausting lives long enough truly to recharge, which prevents them from working, enjoying, and generally existing at the highest level. They barely allow themselves even the smaller breaks necessary throughout the day for proper functioning or even eating well. The trade-off for many people is clear, if unspoken: *My excellent job or career allows me to give my family/loved ones and myself a good life. In return for this, I am willing to sacrifice my physical health, pleasure in the moment, and perhaps even some years of life on the back end.*

Is that not ironic? You do all of this for your family . . . yet you may end up unable to participate in their lives because of your poor health! If it's important to you to be judged a good parent or life partner—as it implicitly seems to be for any person who makes the above trade-off—then how exactly do you earn a decent grade if you are dead and gone for the many years while the kids are growing up?

When highly successful executives from all over the world come to HPI and start comparing their priority lists versus their reality lists, as you did a few pages ago, when they apply their well-honed business skills and thinking to the "business of them," a torrent of emotions typically engulfs them—embarrassment, anger, betrayal of others and of themselves, resentment, disillusionment. Such glaring misalignments in their business world would never be tolerated. Yet somehow, in the area of their life that matters most, the misalignments are given a free pass. The keen, no-nonsense thinking that comprises an indispensible part of their business judgment isn't sufficiently summoned to evaluate the bottom-line reality of their personal lives.

It's always intriguing to hear our clients attempt to rationalize the discrepancy between how they want to live lives based on their deepest values and how they actually live them. Invariably they shock themselves with their flawed, flimsy logic. A common attempt goes like this: "I'm still young enough, I've got time to work all this out. I can't do it right now, but as soon as my life settles down a little, I'll get to the personal stuff."

Think about that. How will the loss of your physical health compromise executing on many of your highest priorities according to that earlier list? If we are willing to invest time and energy in our career and our home, should we not also be willing to invest energy in our body and mind, given that they take precedence over just about everything else?

POSTPONING JOY UNTIL . . . NEVER?

In a 2010 TEDxSydney lecture on work-life balance, business leader and author Nigel Marsh gave his spot-on summation of the thought process of many, many people: "I'll have a life when I retire, when my kids have left home, when my wife has divorced me, my health is failing, I've got no mates or interests left." The line gets a big laugh.

This book speaks, first, to the failure of certain types of achievement to bring a sense of enduring meaning, and second, to the failure of achievement to generate joy in the moment. So many people postpone joy until they have achieved. Too often, though, that moment refuses to come. There's no finish line that tells us, finally, that this particular pursuit is over and now—*now*—is the time to savor it. So we tell ourselves, "Okay, I'll experience happiness at the *next* summit—really." But if you ever say to yourself, "I'll be happy when . . . ," then you can be certain you won't ever feel truly happy: You have the equation backward. The happiness mind-set is faulty— if the accomplishment lacks enduring intrinsic value, or if it's viewed largely as an acquired commodity, not a process, then that happiness is unlikely to come. Ever.

A few years ago, a man in one of our HPI programs raised his hand to tell his story. He was well built, and I knew from his pre-program questionnaire that he was training to be a life coach. "I had it completely wrong," he started boldly, "because from a very young age I bought into the idea that you have to succeed before happiness can come. So I had to experience some kind of demonstrable success. I committed to my goal: win a world championship in boxing. I told myself that if I ever could achieve that, I would be happy because it would mean I was a success in life. Thanks to that belief, I maintained my dedication to the goal, through all my competitions, at every level along the way. I was obsessed. All I could think was that I was going to be someone. Everything else was subverted to that goal. Lo and behold, one day I won a world title. The happiness I felt was unimaginable. Just sensational. But it wasn't exactly what I thought it would feel like; it wasn't profound. Actually, it was more relief than joy. And then what joy I *did* have went away very quickly. For two weeks I sat in my home with this huge trophy and realized that nothing had really changed. I didn't feel very different. The thing I'd been chasing since my adolescence had not transformed me. I felt as if I'd been cheated.

"Then I had a thought: Could it be that I was feeling this way because I was *lucky* to win the title? Yeah, maybe that was it. Winning the title once could easily have been a fluke.

"You won't believe what I did the next morning: I got up and started training to win the title again. You can get lucky once, I thought. Winning it twice can't possibly be luck. No one could doubt you then. All my despair about my lack of satisfaction after winning the title—gone, now that I had a new goal. If I did it twice, I would be somebody, *without question*. I started training like a maniac again."

I've heard a version of this tale from far too many people to count—world-class athletes, executives, mid-level employees in large companies, business owners, doctors and others in medicine. For example: *I didn't feel much satisfaction from completing my master's degree, but I know I will when I get my doctorate; I know I'll feel better about my life when I finally make partner . . . when I finally pass the bar . . . when I earn my CPA; I can't really feel good about myself with a world tennis ranking of 106 . . . when I crack the top 50, I'll start feeling like a success and can really start enjoying my career.* (She did in fact crack the top 50 . . . and nothing changed.) . . . *When I finally get the debt off my back, I can start truly enjoying life . . . one day soon I'll be completely free of financial pressure and can do what makes me happy.* (He sold his business, eliminated all debt, and suddenly became quite wealthy. . . . Within eight months, because of his intense unhappiness, he bought another business, sank deep into debt, and again began his search for happiness and fulfillment.) In his excellent book *The High Price of Materialism*, psychologist Tim Kasser writes, "Before Silicon Graphics, [Netscape founder Jim] Clark said a fortune of $10 million would make him happy; before Netscape, $100 million; before Healtheon, a billion; now, he [says], 'Once I have more money than Larry Ellison, I'll be satisfied.' Ellison, the founder of the software company Oracle, is worth $13 billion."

Such stories remind me of the optical illusion where you look in the center, and it's corkscrewing down and appears to be moving toward something but never gets there. It's endless. It's a trap. *The* trap. The reason so many people suffer through these cycles of Pursuit > Achievement > Dissatisfaction > More Pursuit to Chase Away the Dissatisfaction, ad nauseam, is a fundamentally toxic problem with a certain type of achievement—extrinsic achievement—and the promise of joy and fulfillment it dangles before our eyes. Goals are about the future. But joy is experienced in the present. We use the past to learn, the future to prepare, the present to live. When we lose the present, we lose our lives and all sense of joy.

Here's a very powerful way to become more focused on the present and to avoid constantly postponing happiness until the world around you improves: Simply ask yourself, "If this is as good as it will get for me, how can I find a way to enjoy this time in my life, this very moment, as it exists right now, without change?"

The future always holds more *promise* of joy and fulfillment than the present. Goals are *structures that organize* our preparation for the future, but they rarely, if ever, teach us how to love life *here and now*. Thus the chasing of goals, success, and triumph means, necessarily, either the postponement of joy until that goal is accomplished or experiencing joy in the pursuit itself. The former is the Puritan ethic gone berserk. It's an old story, of course, an ancient story—think of the dad in Harry Chapin's heartbreaking ballad "Cat's in the Cradle" who is so fixated on the future and getting things accomplished that he finally finds the time to be with his son only when the son is unable and unwilling to; or the story of Gene O'Kelly, the late chairman/CEO of KPMG, whose company I led in several workshops, who did not fully get the point of it all until he was diagnosed with terminal brain cancer and was told he had mere months to live. Just how many people out there are obsessed with achieving the next thing, and the one after that? How many people—maybe you?—are, as we speak, so tethered to the future that they are missing it all—the connection to people, the beauty of life, and just about everything that really matters?

Here's one of the major problems with so many of the goals that society has deemed worthy of pursuit: There's always a gap between where you are and where you want to go. This is precisely what generates the vicious cycle of "No matter what I do or achieve, it is never good enough." If, however, the pursuit of your goals is satisfying in itself, then the dissatisfactions associated with achievement might just evaporate. "If work is inherently enjoyable," writes Daniel Pink in his book *Drive*, ". . . then the external inducements at the heart . . . become less necessary." This dynamic extends beyond work.

The sad truth, though, is that when people feel the emptiness of achievement, they take a "brute force" approach: *I'll just do more and more of this until it feels good.* Amazingly few smart people instead stop to wonder:

Could it be that I'm chasing the wrong thing?

CONFLICTING VALUES: WHEN ACHIEVEMENT GOALS COLLIDE

It's vital to get the motivation behind our achievements right, to know what exactly "winning" is supposed to do for us. What is that something that winning is really going to change? Achievement does not happen in a vacuum: Other things unfold during, and as a result of, our pursuit. Often the consequences are unintended and profound. An illuminating example of what I mean is captured in the following experience I once had:

About twenty years ago, not long after the reunification of West and East Germany, I flew into Berlin on a business trip. On the drive to my hotel I got to talking with the cabbie: I asked him how long he'd been driving ("my whole life," he said), which part of Berlin he lived in ("the part that used to be East Berlin"). He'd experienced communism for most of his life and now, finally, he was getting a taste of a vastly different economic and political system. "I've experienced both sides of this with great intensity, yes, and so has my whole family," he said.

"I would love to hear your comparison," I said.

"Well, I'm a little reluctant to tell you because you're an American."

"That's okay," I assured him. "I'm really curious."

"Well," he said, "I didn't have much before—a very modest house. My world was not very complicated. I never worried about feeding my children or having enough to live on. I felt like we'd be fine. I must tell you . . ." He trailed off.

"What?"

"Life was so much more enjoyable then."

"In what way?"

"I had time. I didn't have to race around. I didn't wonder if I would make my house payment. I had rich relationships with people. Life seemed slower, more in the moment."

I just nodded.

"I don't know if I'd go back to the way it was," he continued, "but now I just chase around, I worry all the time about my family, I have no time to spend with friends. I live in a much nicer home. Everything I do and get is of a higher quality, no question. Everything is so much nicer. We used to read about this, but it was not something we hungered for. Yes, I have freedom and I would never trade anything for that. But I long to enjoy my life more and have close, deep relationships the way I used to have. What I really want is to keep the freedom and, at the same time, connect to life as I once did."

I am, most certainly, not endorsing any form of communism. My point is not about communism versus capitalism. Rather, it's about the challenges and responsibilities that come with freedom. My cabbie had ostensibly "won" freedom to pursue new opportunities, a bigger house, nicer things. Something significant was achieved, and he was free to pursue a whole range of things that his new society valued immensely. The indoctrination of what his new society valued, however, collided head-on with cherished core values from his previous world.

We make commitments to ourselves to achieve all kinds of goals, but what about the costs they exact—ones that are so often at least as damaging as the achievement is fulfilling? You'd always wanted to drive a new Mercedes of your own, and finally you made it happen, but by doing so you had to cut back on several extracurricular activities that your children love—e.g., dance lessons, skiing trips, and tennis instruction. You wanted to become general manager of your division, and you finally did, earning the higher salary, more stock options, nicer office, and greater responsibility and respect that come with it . . . but the cost included being on the road more than half the year, losing much of your connection to your kids, and facing divorce. You wanted to become financially independent by the age of forty so you could spend more time with your family . . . but you crossed many ethical lines to make it happen. You went back to your old sales job where you could make considerably more money . . . but it's a culture of heavy drinking and never working out—precisely why you left there in the first place. Your paycheck was much bigger again, but you were back to drinking too much and not exercising.

Perhaps it seems as if I am suggesting that there is an incompatibility between being well off, on the one hand, and living a fulfilling and meaningful life on the other. I do not suggest that all trade-offs are equal. Most every goal we pursue impacts people we care about, for better or worse.

THE CHEATING CULTURE

However we endorse or reject the things our society so publicly values, they aren't all that easy to achieve. They take a lot of energy investment, sometimes a superhuman one. Sometimes they seem to take everything we've got. What happens to the individual who becomes blinded by his or her need to achieve, and whose need morphs into obsession? In such cases—and they happen all the time—the person resorts to practically any strategy to quell the agonizing deficiency.

It's the end, not the means.
It doesn't matter how I get there—as long as I achieve.
Once I succeed, I'm all set, and I won't have to resort again to cheating.
*   That was a one-time deal. . . .*

For the cheater, it's not that simple, of course. There are both short-term and long-term consequences to cheating. I'm pretty sure that no one who's reading this book wants to be remembered as "the person who crossed several ethical lines on his or her way to the top."

Here's a chronology: Darrell (let's call him) pays someone to write his most important high school essays and receives A's on all of them. He cheats on many of his high school math and chemistry tests; again, A's. He pays someone to take the SAT exam using his name, scores in the 98th percentile, and ends up getting into Yale, where he continues his pattern of paying people to do his homework and take the occasional exam. Darrell gets a good job on Wall Street working as a junior analyst for a high-profile financial services firm.

He'd be set for life, if only he weren't set for a huge fall.

Throughout this whole ascension, Darrell feels like a fraud. He didn't earn the competence he is supposed to possess. He feels like he's in over his head now, as he should: He lacks the math and writing skills required for his job. He always feels under siege, though there's no one to whom he can or will admit it, or why. He resigns from his analyst position before he gets fired; he was clearly unhappy, as was his employer. He starts working for his father's marketing firm and hates that, too. He lacks true self-esteem. He's deeply unhappy.

Not everyone pays to cheat. There are less steep slopes. For some, what begins as simply padding expenses—inflating charges on taxi receipts, exaggerating mileage claims between clients, putting in for cab rides or meals that never happened, etc.—evolves, say, into occasionally charging personal airline tickets to the company charge card. If discovered, you'll apologize for the honest mistake—but your company's accounting department is so disorganized that you're sure no one will ever figure it out. Or maybe you offer sizable cash discounts for services that will never get entered in the company books, thus providing yourself with significant tax-free income.

There are versions of people like this all over the place—and why wouldn't there be? The pressure to succeed is enormous, at times unbearable—in business, sports, academics, government, the arts, and even in one's community. If you're trying to make the team, and you've worked honestly while the guys at the lockers left and right of you have been juicing, what chance do you have unless you cheat, too? In a poll of American teens listed in *Who's Who Among American High School Students*—many of the country's best and brightest—four in five said that they had cheated at least once during their high school career. Lawyers are pressured to increase their billable hours, salespeople to meet their quotas. Maybe you're a car salesperson, a stockbroker, a multilevel marketing distributor, a CFO or CEO or politician or pharmaceutical rep or police officer, and lots of people otherwise just like you are pinching here and there. These high expectations can exert a lot of pressure to stretch the truth or to bend reality (maybe even just a tiny bit) to achieve career success.

It's not that people are bad. Sometimes it truly *is* the system that's largely at fault. Research has shown that "rewarding employees for achieving narrow goals such as exact production quantities may encourage them to neglect other areas, take undesirable 'ends justify the means' risks, or . . . engage in more unethical behavior than they would otherwise." Business and the larger society are set up in such a way that honest people may suffer from what is known as "motivated blindness."

That's why, if you lack a foundation of sufficient character, the forces of society may simply prove too much. And then what was once unthinkable becomes quite normal and accepted practice. The pull to the dark side most often occurs an inch at a time, under the radar of one's conscience—that's how it appeared to happen to Jayson

Blair, the *New York Times* journalist fired for fabricating news stories. That's how it happens to many corrupt politicians (the list is voluminous): They generally didn't start out as cynics or compromisers or outright thieves. That's how it happened to Scott Sullivan, who was awarded the "CFO Excellence Award" by *CFO* magazine in 1998 and then, four years later, was fired from WorldCom in the midst of allegations of massive fraud. Sullivan's gradual addiction to a life of luxury opened the door to his cooking the books and eventually one of the most infamous corporate implosions in the history of American business.

When the goal is simply to win, to achieve, then cheating becomes tolerable; indeed, necessary; indeed, practically recommended. If the goal is to win, then everything is for sale, even your soul, for the right price. What once was unthinkable—going over to the dark side—is now absolutely thinkable. There's a willingness, as David Callahan writes in his book *The Cheating Culture*, "to make the wrong choices, at least when it comes to money and career."

Is all cheating the same? No and yes. In the movie *Casablanca*, when Rick (Humphrey Bogart) has his roulette man in the backroom casino cheat, but does so to help a couple in distress (plus, the person he's cheating out of money is himself), Rick hardly needs to rationalize his actions. But wait: Those who cheat often have a handy rationalization at their disposal: *I'm doing it so we as a family can succeed.* If the intention is good, if the ethical violation was for a good cause or for righting a perceived injustice, then we can feel completely justified or exonerated in our ignoble action. Character, it is said, is who you are when nobody's looking. Cheating is also something you do when nobody's looking.

WHAT HAPPENS IF YOU DON'T ACHIEVE?

You can achieve something that exacts too high a cost. Yet you're so addicted to achievement that you continue to pursue similar goals, or the same goal over and over, somehow convincing yourself that *this time* your triumph won't fail to provide psychological, emotional, and spiritual nourishment.

But what happens when you pursue success . . . and simply fail to get it? When achievement is how you build your sense of value, what do you do with failure?

Failure to achieve can have devastating consequences. Not achieving your goals may leave you feeling fragile, like an impostor. It is a somewhat bitter trick that achieving society's goals can often leave you feeling empty . . . and *not* achieving society's goals can leave you feeling empty, too.

It's clearly lose-lose.

This is what I mean when I say that character building is the only way to win. If success at external things doesn't really matter (to a great extent), then failure at such things shouldn't matter, either. What matters is the person you are becoming as a consequence of the pursuit, and character must be at the heart of everything you do and are.

At our HPI headquarters we have a small elite tennis academy where young boys and girls between the ages of ten and eighteen train very hard five days a week to become world-class players. Tennis is a very demanding sport. Players are all alone and have no time-outs; matches can last literally hours, and the scoring system in tennis promotes mounting pressure. There are countless opportunities for cheating, an expensive cost of admission—court time, racquets, balls, shoes, instruction, travel to tournaments, etc.—and rivalries can become bigger than life. Day one of their training, academy participants are told the following:

At this academy, we use the demands and stress of elite tennis to most importantly help you become strong, resilient people of great character. We care about your tennis but we care more about who you are becoming because of tennis. Our most important imperative at this academy is winning with character. Every day represents another opportunity to grow in self-control, respect for others, persistence, positivity and trust-worthiness. No matter how far you go as a player, if you use tennis to strengthen character, tennis will always be a priceless gift.

The simple act of re-purposing tennis to become a vehicle for ac-celerating character development gives meaning and value to all the years of training whether or not the goal to play professional tennis ever becomes realized. The fact is that any achievement goal can be re-purposed to become an opportunity to grow strengths of char-acter. Regardless of whether one succeeds or fails in the external achievement itself, something of real value will have been gained.

Now let's examine how this all got started in the first place.

2

How Did We Get Here?

*They were so strong in their beliefs that there came a time when it
hardly mattered what exactly those beliefs were.*

—Louise Erdrich

The first days, first months, first years of life tend to go something like this:

The infant smiles for the first time . . . and her parents go crazy. The baby utters his first word, the toddler takes her first step, the child gets his first A in school . . . and the parents lavish the child with approval, kisses, signs of pleasure. Naturally, the child feels valued. The same sequence plays out following the first soccer goal, the first appearance on the honor roll, the first job, first date, first major academic degree, etc.

Nothing wrong with any of that. All these milestones, however, are *external* markers of value.

From the daily paper to *People* magazine to reality TV to countless websites and blogs covering business news, fashion, celebrity, sports, and more, the bulk of attention is paid to a certain kind of visible achievement, and there is a simple linear quality to each achievement: the more tangible, the better; the more remarkable, the better; the more difficult, the better. Climb local mountain, good; climb Mount

Everest, much better; climb Mount Everest in winter, fantastic! At work, attention is paid to—and one is literally paid for—how many hours one works, how much revenue one's department makes, how many billable hours one racks up, how many promotions one earns, how many direct reports one can count, etc. Shine in these areas, and others are impressed by the success—even, to an extent, blinded by it. *Achievement itself* becomes the measuring stick, and opportunities to be sought, challenges to be engaged are everywhere.

Much harder to spot are the deeper more subtle markers of accomplishment—for example, integrity, effort, compassion, generosity, humility, trustworthiness. They're out there, for sure, but they receive far less public attention. These character strengths are noticed and admired privately by some, publicly celebrated by few.

If society's lifelong habit of first and foremost valuing visible accomplishments has its origins in our very first days, then let's be clear about the earliest shapers of this emerging worldview: parents. Parents constantly influence what their children think, like, and dislike. Because this influence is profound and ongoing, parents are the leading influencers not only of what dreams their children embrace, but also of their children's grown-up dreams. Is it natural for a grade schooler to say, as I've heard more than once, "I want to play professional football when I grow up"? Is it natural for a child to say, "I want to be a millionaire"? For good or bad, as you will see, this is the result of an indoctrination process that shapes, at an early age, our perception of success.

This does not mean that every household, or even most, are hotbeds of materialism, vanity, and self-absorption. Far from it. Most parents, I'd propose, are intent on promoting proper values. In his book *Character Matters*, Thomas Lickona writes, "The family is the first school of virtue. It is where we learn about love." When asked, "Who or what has been the greatest influence on your becoming a person of strong character?" the overwhelming majority of respondents say their parents. Nor does this mean that all external achievement is rooted in suspect values. In his book *The Millionaire Mind,*

Thomas J. Stanley, Ph.D., randomly selected 733 millionaires and asked them to name the factors that contributed to their success. The number one factor? Integrity. True, they were giving answers about their own success, but there are many other, eminently reasonable answers (persistence, ambition, focus, work ethic, self-confidence) they might have given.

For all the attempts parents make to ground their own lives and that of their children's in virtue, perhaps the bigger, more problematical tide of influence is that of society. It is seductive. It is incessant. Its reach is inescapable. The imagery of success exemplified in commercials, advertisements, TV shows, movies, and online is the ideal, and the ideal becomes the standard. And as goes society, so go its individual members, and vice versa, each reflecting the other's values. If one is inclined to act counter to the values of one's culture, it requires an almost superhuman effort. For now, in a sense, the die is cast. There is little room for rebellion. "The proper time to influence the character of a child," wrote William R. Inge, "is about a hundred years before he's born."

SOCIETY, THUS, HAS ESTABLISHED an invisible but nonetheless very present "scorecard," one in which Money, Status, Power, and Beauty are the bold-faced rubrics.★ It aids us in building, directing, and validating our sense of worth, which in turn strongly influences the choices we make about what to invest our energy in.

It's fairly clear, I think, that no matter how independent-minded we think we are, this scorecard affects almost all of us profoundly.

As we follow our ambition, we may become transfixed by the goals we are racing to achieve, goals we might never have chosen but for the existence and influence of that scorecard. According to Bonnie

---

★ In some parts of the world, including the U.S., another rubric would be Hard Work. According to Adam Okulicz-Kozaryn, author of "Europeans Work to Live and American Live to Work," a 2010 paper published in the *Journal of Happiness Studies*, Americans believe more strongly than Europeans that hard work and success are linked.

Ware, an Australian writer and musician who spent years working in palliative care, treating patients who had gone home to die, so she got to know them intimately in their final weeks, by far the most commonly expressed regret was "I wish I'd had the courage to live a life true to myself, not the life others expected of me."

With startling ease, we can find ourselves chained to the goals that have been imposed on us. In a sense, the indoctrination we are all subject to makes us victims of a form of "identity theft," though a far more toxic brand of it than we usually mean by that term. Instead of a stranger hijacking our ATM card number to reroute money from our bank account, someone or something has taken control of the value proposition we use to judge the success of our lives. In doing so, they have stolen the great bulk of our energy and time, with no possibility of compensation for our loss.

Oh, and one more thing: Rather than a stranger stealing our identity, the persons enabling this tragic theft, day after day and year after year, are those closest to us. When those we most trust instruct this, we fail to rally resistance. And one day we begin the same process with our children.

WAIT—WHY DO WE WANT TO ACHIEVE IN THE FIRST PLACE?

Perhaps we're getting ahead of ourselves. Why are we so achievement-oriented? What—as actors often ask—is our motivation? Is it to keep up with the Joneses? Is it to make others happy?

Since we spend so much of our waking lives in the pursuit of various things, then surely it would help a little to understand the why behind it.

The why is at once highly complex and exceedingly simple. One reason for why we wish to achieve is that we want to please others— our parents, earliest and foremost. Later, there are others we wish to please. Our reasons to achieve are both conscious and not conscious. They can be positive—wishing to achieve a constructive outcome (for example, to grow)—or negative—wishing to avoid a destructive outcome (for example, not to disappoint others). Our positive reasons are often called "approach" goals, our negative reasons "avoidance" goals.

The reasons may also be divided into categories of intrinsic and extrinsic. Simply put, intrinsic motivation means that one can enjoy and be interested in an activity for its own sake. Extrinsic motivation refers to behavior that is enacted for some motive outside the activity itself. Extrinsic motivation typically involves external regulation wherein an individual seeks to obtain an external reward or avoid an external punishment.

What is it about our understanding of achievement that may be faulty—or at least more complicated than typically believed?

By understanding how many of our beliefs are false, or only partly true, we may once and for all free ourselves of that mind-set created in us when we were very young, one characterized by a subtle and powerful drive to endlessly pursue goals that will prove that we are winners.

THE MYTH OF SELF-ESTEEM

"I do not know the key to success," Bill Cosby once said, "but I know the key to failure: Make everybody happy."

Much has been written in recent years about the veritable self-esteem industry that has emerged over the past generation or two, particularly in the United States. So central is the notion of self-esteem to defining ourselves and others, both adults and children, that one might reasonably suggest that people come in really three types: those with insufficient or damaged self-esteem (their sense of self-worth is fragile), those with a bit too much self-esteem (narcissists), and those precious few among us with just the right amount of self-esteem. "The Three Little Bears," therapist's version.

The inclination to protect our self-esteem is a potent force. We've come to believe that self-esteem is to the psyche as the heart or brain is to the body: the thing without which the larger organism simply cannot function. To build and protect their self-esteem, people engage in a wide range of behaviors, some functional, some dysfunctional. Achieving goals, we tell ourselves, is one of the best ways to strengthen our self-esteem. We all want more of it because it will surely makes us feel good. Let's grow it, even if we sometimes overshoot the mark and grow too much of it.

There's just one problem with this view. It's not true. Higher self-esteem does not lead to better performance. Higher self-esteem does not cause higher grades. The latest research shows that high self-esteem is not connected to leadership; nor, at the other end, is low self-esteem connected to violence, smoking, drinking, or taking drugs. One of the only positives is the connection researchers have found between high self-esteem and self-reported feelings of happiness.

As researchers currently understand it, then, high self-esteem is not necessarily the panacea it was thought to be.

How can this be? It makes no sense. Don't we all know someone with damaged self-esteem who is incapable of fulfilling his or her dreams because of that one fatal flaw?

The problem with self-esteem as it is judged and cultivated today is both how much of it one may "possess" and how it was built. Was it built on a series of victories? Not good: It can just as easily topple with a series of losses. It's a tenuous self-esteem, and if it falls (more likely *when* it falls) is something out of one's control.

Was the self-esteem built on early success that one has doggedly sought not to challenge, for fear that it's all a house of cards? Not good, either. Defensiveness always betrays insecurity and fragility. Self-esteem that cannot be tested reveals instability. Students who based their self-esteem on academic competence, report Crocker,

Brook, Niya, and Villacorta, avoided practice so they could attribute failure to lack of practice, not lack of ability.

Was the self-esteem built on excessive praise? If so, then it's a very tottering kind of self-esteem, indeed. Excessive praise represents a distortion of reality. Non-reality-based feedback produces non-reality-based self-esteem. "What kind of man makes it through Hell Week?" writes Lieutenant Commander Eric Greitens, a SEAL in the U.S. Navy Reserve and author of *The Heart and the Fist: The Education of a Humanitarian, the Making of a Navy SEAL*. "That's hard to say. But I do know—generally—who won't make it. There are a dozen types that fail: the weight-lifting meatheads who think that the size of their biceps is an indication of their strength, the kids covered in tattoos announcing to the world how tough they are, the preening leaders who don't want to get dirty, and the look-at-me former athletes who have always been told they are stars but have never been pushed beyond the envelope of their talent to the core of their character. In short, those who fail are the ones who focus on show. The vicious beauty of Hell Week is that you either survive or fail, you endure or you quit, you do—or you do not."

Any self-esteem, high or low, that is *contingent* on something beyond one's control breaks easily. Studies show that the energy one invests in particular activities is, not surprisingly, directly related to the basis for one's self-esteem. So, for example, the amount of time one spends grooming, shopping, partying, and socializing is predicted by how much one's self-esteem is based on appearance. If your self-esteem is based on academic performance, then how much time you spent studying can be predicted. Janelle Cambron and Linda Acitelli reported in *The Journal of Social and Clinical Psychology* that individuals who strongly base their self-esteem on the quality of their friendships reported greater needs for approval and reassurance, were more sensitive to negative feedback, and were more prone to depression than individuals who do not base their self-esteem on the quality of their friendships. The same is true for other metrics, including more explicitly constructive endeavors: So for those who base their self-esteem on virtue, the time they spend on volunteer activities may be predicted. People develop "contingency beliefs"—the idea that feelings about oneself are dependent on meeting some standard of excellence; in short, "if-thens"—that must be met before one can qualify as having value.

SELF-ESTEEM IS NOT A BASIC NEED

Does this make the whole notion of self-esteem a myth? No, not when it's built on something internal. Right now, though, there is no real connection between self-esteem, on the one hand, and, on the other, the most essential aspect of ourselves: character. Self-esteem and character can be completely independent of each other. Someone can have high self-esteem—extraordinarily high self-esteem even—while also being a highly unethical individual. From sports to politics, from business to law, daily headlines chronicle colossal character collapses from individuals exuding high self-esteem—e.g., John Edwards, Tiger Woods, Mark McGwire, Marion Jones, John Ensign, Bernie Madoff, Leona Helmsley, Arnold Schwarzenegger.

Thanks to the self-esteem craze, there seems to be no lack of narcissists these days. A person may be damaged when he or she is heaped with lavish praise for meeting or exceeding performance expectations: "You're the greatest," "You're so gifted," "I love you so much when you do what I know you can do," "I'm so proud of you," etc. Granted unconditionally, this kind of attention and approval will more often than not lead to long-term negative consequences. It's bad for the individual and bad for the culture at large. The enabled, entitled narcissist believes he or she is deserving of everything. This notion was comically embodied by a character on the TV show *30 Rock*, played by Jon Hamm. This character was so classically handsome, and had received so much praise and attention throughout his life for his looks, that he had taken this inflated sense of self into mid-adulthood and grown into a terrible tennis player, an awful cook, a dangerous motorcyclist, and a pediatrician who should never have been granted a license to practice. Yet no one had the heart to tell him he was atrocious at all these things. The larger culture also suffers when praise is passed around like after-dinner mints. It's no coincidence, I think, that the U.S. Army's recruiting slogan for a generation—"Be all you can be"—was replaced in 2001 by the decidedly anti-teamwork-tinged "Army of One." (In 2006 it was replaced by "Army Strong.") By numerous measures, it is an age of excessive self-preoccupation and, ultimately, unreality. The writer Fran Lebowitz addressed precisely this when she caustically told a group of young writers, "There are too many books, the books are terrible, and it's because *you* have been taught to have self-esteem." Tom Wolfe coined the phrase the "Me Generation" for those coming of age in the 1970s; one wonders what phrase he would need to come up with for a large portion of today's culture.

Whether you have high self-esteem or low, one of the key considerations is the external nature of it. Failure to achieve a targeted external outcome can devastate one's sense of value. You didn't make the starting five on your high school basketball team your senior year, you didn't make partner in your law firm by age forty-five, you didn't make the Olympic team in your final year of competition, etc. You did your best and your best wasn't good enough. You spent ten years of your life trying to become a professional golfer, and now it's obvious that all that work, sacrifice, and pain were for nothing. So now you deeply resent all the time sacrificed to golf, a lost decade of sweat and toil. Considering all the money spent, all the time away from friends and family, all the investment of energy, you get deeply saddened and regretful. From your perspective, the goal wasn't achieved, so the ten years were nothing but a tragic waste! The feeling of worthlessness drives people to seek out . . . yet *more* external achievements to confirm their value. Such a cycle usually fails, of course. Ask the championship boxer.

YOUR WORST FEARS ARE CONFIRMED

When your scorecard for building self-esteem is purely achievement-based, winning changes little in terms of building self-worth. When you lose, your deepest fears are confirmed: You are the sorry incompetent you always suspected you were. Confidence deteriorates with every failure. Your self-esteem suffers a major hit every time you don't reach the desired mark. You dread the thought of putting yourself on the competitive line again for fear of failing again. When your mask of achievement has been lifted, you're not sure who you are. Are you anything? If your value is made possible largely via goal achievement, then who are you when you fail to achieve?

The fact is, for a generation now we have gotten self-esteem wrong. According to Jean Twenge, Ph.D., author of *Generation Me* and coauthor of *The Narcissism Epidemic*, "self-esteem is an outcome, not a cause." Dr. Roy Baumeister, professor of psychology at Florida State University and a towering figure in the study of self-esteem, has said, "After all these years, I'm sorry to say, my recommendation is to forget about self-esteem and concentrate more on self-control and self-discipline." The notions that self-esteem can be earned externally and, in the case of the narcissist, that it needn't be earned at all are both seriously flawed.

After considering all the evidence in my years of experience, here is what I've come to believe: Stable, healthy self-esteem is contingent, first, on the energy and time one expends to build specific character strengths—e.g., kindness, gratefulness, persistence—and, second, on the alignment of one's energy and behavior with highly specific, enduring personal values.

If our prevailing view of self-esteem has been largely misguided, then what else might we have gotten wrong about achievement? Could it be that the kinds of achievement that we have long thought brought the most spectacular returns—earning millions, living in the biggest house, acquiring the most prestigious titles, etc.—are in fact nearly meaningless when it comes to determining how to live a truly "successful" life? Could it be that, for instance, parental practices encouraging just this kind of achievement might in fact completely undermine intrinsic motivation?

Yes, it could. In a study conducted by the University of Rochester, psychologists asked 246 adults to evaluate the importance of six life goals: physical health, growing and learning new things, helping others improve their lives, wealth, the admiration of many, and desirable appearance. The first three goals, you may note, are by most standards rather wholesome; the last three, less so. After a year, the researchers checked up on the subjects to see how well they had done in achieving their goals, as well as how happy and healthy they were. Those who had focused on the first three goals felt great. Not so for the other group. For those who pursued fame, money, and beauty, there was no relationship between their mood and what they achieved. None. Interestingly, the more success achieved for the last three goals, the more *negative* the correlation: greater anxiety, depressed mood, and health problems.

How *do* we build value, then? Carol Dweck has done pioneering work on the primacy of effort in determining outlook: If you've earned a grade honestly—whatever that grade may be—then you genuinely increase your sense of personal integrity. Jennifer Crocker and Lora Park argue that the path a person chooses to build self-esteem is a critical consideration; it's how people validate their sense of value. "Pursuing self-esteem by being virtuous, compassionate, generous or altruistic," they write, "would seem to have fewer costs."

While I agree with what Dweck, Crocker, and Park, and many others in this field have posited, I believe the answer lies beyond even that. *True self-esteem can really be built only on the basis of enduring character strengths*, both "performance" and "moral" (see graphic on page 42)—and the moral family of strengths must take precedence over the performance family of strengths. Moral character strengths define the values that govern our relationships with others, while performance strengths pertain to the values that govern our relationships with ourselves. Achievement devoid of moral value can lead to ruth-lessness, even cruelty.

As depicted in the pyramid graphic, human beings possess physical needs, emotional needs, mental needs, and spiritual needs. Anyone who has ever taken an introductory-level psychology course will note that this pyramid is reminiscent of Abraham Maslow's "hierarchy of needs" pyramid. HPI's pyramid "builds" on Maslow's idea, modeling not just these needs but also the way in which they will be satisfied. Physical needs are positioned at the base of the pyramid because they are foundational to healthy development and personal fulfillment. The higher one moves up the pyramid, the more important the needs are for optimizing personal happiness and healthy development.

The Hierarchy of Character Strengths

Spiritual
Needs

Love and Care for Others, Kindness,
Truthfulness, Integrity, Humility, Gratefulness,
Justice, Fairness, Generosity, Compassion,
Respect for Others, Patience with Others, Honor

Moral
Character
Strengths

Mental
Needs

Wisdom, Critical Thinking,
Concentration, Seeking Challenges,
Creativity, Self-Control, Decisiveness,
Punctuality, Adaptability

Performance
Character
Strengths

Emotional
Needs

Optimism, Hope, Determination, Courage, Positivity, Love of
Learning, Confidence, Ambition, Competitiveness, Diligence,
Resiliency, Humor, Self-Compassion, Patience with Self

Physical
Needs

Food, Sleep, Hydration, Exercise, Movement, etc.

And how does one achieve this optimal state of well-being—or "self-actualization," as Maslow called his apex? Performance character strengths assist in meeting emotional and mental needs, while moral character strengths assist in meeting spiritual needs.

The distinction between external and internal contingencies for building self-esteem is a critical one. An attempt to build self-esteem on the back of external outcomes, when one clearly has little or no direct control over the results, will lead to unstable feelings of self-worth. In contrast, an attempt to build self-esteem on internal contingencies such as humility, effort, optimism, dedication, etc.—things well within the sphere of a person's control—*can* and almost inevitably *will* lead to a more secure, healthy sense of self. When the ultimate goal for becoming a business professional, doctor, or for climbing Mount Everest is internally driven, when such a pursuit is valued primarily for the opportunity it provides for building enduring character traits, then failure to reach the external goal is of considerably lesser account. What *does* matter is the impact of the pursuit on your character. Have you become more ethical, principle-centered, humble, respectful of others, grateful? Have you become less of these? Did you cheat, take shortcuts, and disrespect others when you didn't get the results you wanted? Did you deepen and sharpen those moral character traits that someday, when people talk about you and your legacy, you'd want them to talk about?

Self-esteem is not a birthright. It must be earned. It must hinge on things over which one has control—persistence, hope, generosity, kindness, and such. In this way, one can invest time and energy very deliberately in the direction one wishes. According to theorists Edward L. Deci and Richard M. Ryan, true self-esteem develops when one's actions are congruent with one's inner core of values and beliefs rather than reflections of externally or internally imposed demands. It is that kind of self-esteem, quite simply, that transcends anything that Society's Scorecard demands of us.

ADDICTED TO ACHIEVEMENT:
THE CHEMISTRY WE CAN'T ESCAPE

Extrinsic rewards can never fully satisfy. This assertion, proven again and again with high performers I've worked with, sounds like an opinion, but it is not merely an ideological position that I, and others, have staked out. It's a conclusion based on pure science. Addiction to achievement has a physiological, neurochemical basis, as real and compelling as addiction to drugs, food, gambling, sex, etc. The craving/short-term pleasure cycle is roughly the same. In each case, the acquisition of the desire increases dopamine, a neurotransmitter that activates receptors in a particular area of the brain called the *nucleus accumbens*. One can understand the use of the term "rush" when referring to the feeling one gets: As Daniel Pink puts it in *Drive*, "The mechanism of most addictive drugs is to send a fusillade of dopamine to the nucleus accumbens." The surge raises dopamine levels to three to five times what is considered normal, thus providing relief and pleasure. Dopamine, along with the two other brain hormones serotonin and noradrenaline, are often referred to as the "happy messengers." In this sense, one might think that dopamine acts, in part, as a naturally occurring drug that contributes to our happiness and then (as we'll see) undermines it, but its broader function is to spur us to learn new behaviors so that we might maximize rewards. Dopamine's numerous functions in the brain extend far beyond just these areas of motivation, reward, and punishment. It also plays a key role in cognition, voluntary movement, sleep, mood, attention, working memory, and lactation.

All rewards and behaviors, even everyday ones like eating and exercising, have the potential to become addictions when dopamine levels increase as a consequence of the repeated activity. As with other addictions, the pleasure of external achievement never lasts. The new, improved, pleasing state gradually becomes the normal state and the dopamine neurons cease to fire. "Our neurons quickly adapt to the pleasure of high-definition television, or that fancy new car, or the softness of the cashmere sweater," explains science writer Jonah Lehrer in "Shopping, Depression and Dopamine." The burst of joy, excitement, and pleasure recedes like the tide (called "dopamine ergil adaptation") and we start taking it for granted. To get the same rush—or fix, if you will—we must push closer to the edge, take more risks, go where we've never been before. Psychologists Philip Brickman and Donald Campbell famously dubbed this phenomenon—in which we tend to return to a previous, rather fixed level of happiness (or unhappiness) despite the small and even big ups and downs of life—"the hedonic treadmill." As it applies to extrinsic achievement, it's clear that there can never be enough shopping, trophies, money, home renovations, cosmetic surgery fixes, rare jewelry, famous artworks, etc., to make a meaningful, enduring difference; this is why the very wealthy, who can buy anything they want, are quite often no happier than the rest of us.

This need to achieve can easily be seen in the words of Karl, a fifty-two-year-old executive attending HPI, who had succeeded spectacularly at every level from high school through his current position as CFO of a large multinational corporation: "I'm never satisfied with my accomplishments. I always push for more. No matter what I do, it never seems enough to bring me sustained happiness." In his recent memoir, *Stories I Only Tell My Friends*, actor Rob Lowe recounts the letdown he felt soon after landing the biggest role of his then-young career. "Truth be told, after the long, adrenaline-filled audition process, I'm also feeling a little let down. (I will later learn this is a hallmark of alcoholism; we call it the Peggy Lee Syndrome. You reach a goal you've been striving for, only to feel 'Is that all there is?')"

Thus, the need for another fix is always just around the corner and the obsession to achieve continues unabated. There is simply never enough. "We are wired to always want more no matter how much we already have," writes Lehrer. We are, if you will, achievement junkies, always chasing something external for that next dopamine hit.

As with any real addiction, breaking the habit is no easy task, because the roots of the addiction are neurochemical.

Are we all susceptible? Equally susceptible? There is evidence that vulnerability to addiction varies from individual to individual, depending on the density of dopamine receptor cells, particularly D2 cells, in the nucleus accumbens. (There are five such receptor types—D1, D2, D3, D4, and D5.) Evidence is mounting that addiction involves an array of specific neurotransmitter genes including serotonin. Serotonin impacts mood, impulsivity, aggressiveness, and irritability, thus the level of serotonin in the brain affects our perception and experience of reward, which contributes to potentially addictive behavior. It appears that those with fewer D2 receptors in the nucleus accumbens may have an increased risk of addiction and obsession. Why? If you have fewer D2 receptors, then you require a more intense stimulus before you can feel the satisfaction of reward. Researchers refer to this as "reward sensitivity" or "reward deferring syndrome." Alcoholics have fewer D2 receptors. The more obese a person, the lower their predicted number of D2 receptors.

To sum up, if achievement is rewarded by the release of dopamine, then achievement becomes addictive in and of itself. Movement toward the goal triggers dopamine release, while movement away from the goal causes it to stop. The mere expectation of achievement (goal setting) becomes integrated into one's sense of self. Achievement becomes part of our identity (known as the "endowment effect"). In short, achievement serves as the trigger for our own internal form of substance abuse—a self-induced dopamine addiction. To quote Christopher Lasch, "Drugs are merely the most obvious form of addiction in our society."

Suppose, however, we could get our dopamine neurons firing in response to acts of kindness, generosity, or courage—things over which we had some control—even a great deal of control? Wouldn't that be a very good thing?

PART II

THE NEW PERFORMANCE SCORECARD

3

The Cry for a New Scorecard

"You're gonna need a bigger boat."
—Chief Martin Brody in *Jaws*

We care about being happy. We're fascinated about what's behind happiness. We just haven't been all that successful in achieving it.

Over the last generation, and particularly over the last decade or so, there has been a torrent of studies about well-being* by those in numerous academic disciplines, especially behavioral and social science; an explosion of interest in these ideas by the general population; and a deluge of accessible books inspired by all this research. Do these studies tell us anything new and conclusive about happiness? Absolutely. They have provided grist for the mills of economists, anthropologists, psychologists, even policy makers. British prime minister David Cameron has backed funding for a study of the well-being of his people, to provide another way—perhaps a better way—to measure the country's "health" than just GDP. The nation's official happiness index is expected in 2012.

---

* The term preferred by the research community—though I use "happiness" and "well-being" interchangeably.

Among the hundreds of studies, something approaching a consensus has emerged about what generally makes, or keeps, people happy:

- connection to others
- close companionship
- positive relationships
- rich spiritual commitment and meaning
- marriage
- having personal control
- being extroverted
- generosity
- being hopeful

That's not to say that if you possess one or more of these traits you will be happy, or that if you don't possess one or more you won't be. An individual who isn't married, for instance, would not necessarily be happier married; nor is someone who is married necessarily happier than he or she would be if not. At least one study found that marriage's salutary effect on happiness is temporary, a boost that lasts roughly two years. But these traits have been shown, time and again, to be excellent indicators of well-being across a population. The more positive relationships one has, for instance, the likelier one is to feel a sense of value; the more one is cut off from others, the more one's sense of value is compromised.

Yet as much as the above list may seem unsurprising, there are still some fundamental things that many of us seem not to get. Take generosity, for instance. Its effect on well-being has not been studied in great detail—certainly not when compared, say, to the effect of wealth on well-being. For that, so many theories abound that it's hard to know exactly what to believe: Most studies say money doesn't matter, or not that much, anyway. Others say it matters but only up to a certain annual income level sufficient to meet one's most basic needs. Another study points out that one-third of people with assets of $10 million or more said that money brought more problems than it solved.

But what of generosity? We're now learning some useful things about this character strength, though the insights might, at first, seem as common sense as those of a study that concludes that sitting outside in winter in a bathing suit makes you feel cold. A 2008 study, as an example, showed that while spending on oneself did not correlate with a person's happiness, spending on others and charity did, significantly so.

Hardly shocking, right? Yet a study of college students showed that the seemingly obvious equation above is hardly obvious at all. Most of the participants "thought personal spending would make them happier than pro-social spending." In a second experiment with college students, researchers gave participants either a $5 or $20 bill and instructed half the students to spend it by that evening on themselves and the other half to spend it by that evening on others. The latter group "reported feeling happier at the end of the day than those who spent the money on themselves."

I find that not at all surprising.

Perhaps we're not as *aware* of what makes us happy as we think we are. Or we know perfectly well what makes us happy and for some reason we're not sufficiently motivated to make the necessary change. After all, why, if it takes all of $5 a day spent on other people to make us happier, wouldn't we all proactively be doing it every day?★

In her excellent book *The How of Happiness*, psychology professor Sonja Lyubomirsky chronicles things people do that make them happy. Be grateful, for one: An astonishing 94 percent of people who recount three good things that happened each day feel significant depression relief after fifteen days. She cites another study that shows that people who are consistently grateful report being relatively happier and more energetic. And perhaps this is a key—*the*

★ This is hardly the only case of human beings not doing what they assuredly know is good for them. As Daniel Pink points out in *Drive*, "We don't save enough for retirement even though it's to our clear economic advantage to do so."

key?—to a successful marriage: Spend five minutes each day expressing gratitude for everything your partner has done for you.

Another trait that strongly correlates with happiness: compassion. Its value to us is so widely understood that popular bumper stickers—COMMIT RANDOM ACTS OF KINDNESS—and the Dalai Lama—"Making other people happy is true happiness"—have pretty much the same thing to say about it.

Compassion for others may have its roots in self-compassion, and researchers have found a strong link between high self-compassion and happiness. According to Kristin Neff, professor of human development at the University of Texas at Austin, self-compassion offers the happiness benefit of high self-esteem but without the consequences. In the words of Paul Gilbert, clinical psychologist and author of *The Compassionate Mind*, "If you have a kind, encouraging, supporting part to you, you'll be OK. If you have a bully that kicks you every time you fall over, then you're going to struggle."

Lyubomirsky also points out that of the main determinants of happiness, a mere 10 percent is largely circumstantial—one's social class, looks, health, etc.—while 40 percent is "intentional activity"—what we do and think. The remaining 50 percent is dependent on our own biological (or "hedonic") set point that is coded in our genes. What's important is that as much as 40 percent of your happiness is under your own control, and that can make all the difference.

The massive body of research we now have in this area all points, despite variations in particulars here and there, to the same thing: *meaning.* "Our souls are not hungry for fame, comfort, wealth or power," writes author and rabbi Harold Kushner. "Our souls are hungry for meaning, for the sense that we have figured out how to live so that our lives matter." Poets and spiritual leaders have said this for millennia, and now neuroscientists and economists are saying it. The research produced by the brilliant men and women of both hard science and social science has taken us a good deal down the road we ultimately want to go down—to understand the connection between meaning and well-being, and then actually to embody it and enjoy it.

But I believe they have not taken us all the way. For the last generation or so, there has been great focus on many key issues such as self-esteem, work/life balance, living in the present, religious enlightenment, and others. In a crucial way, though, the circle has not been closed. If, in the short life we have, we are going to create value—a sense of significance and meaning—then we must create not only a secure foundation and a plan that guides its building and maintenance, but something more. Something that has yet to be fully defined in all the research that's been conducted thus far. Without this piece, it becomes subtly so very difficult for us to determine how to live the best, most fulfilling life we can. That piece is the primacy of purpose.

PURPOSE: YOUR ULTIMATE MISSION

Without purpose, we can do nothing truly meaningful; our actions have no real point to them. Without purpose, everything is a struggle and we naturally expend the least energy possible.

The most sacred thing we have as human beings is our sense of purpose. It's what separates us from all other species. Our capacity to ask why is the evolutionary masterpiece that enables us to create meaning for our pursuits, including *those that, on the surface, appear to be extrinsic*. Purpose does not, in fact, negate or trivialize our external achievements—the making of money (even lots of it), the climbing of professional ladders, the acquisition of trophies, etc. It gives these "interim" achievements context. By doing this, purpose ultimately helps to focus us to achieve with even greater energy. When Andre Agassi finally converged on his true purpose, he suddenly found use and value for many of the external achievements for which he had once had such contempt. "At last my fame will have a purpose," he wrote, seemingly at peace.

We use a pyramid graphic at the Institute to show the primacy of purpose. As human beings we begin at the base of the pyramid and proceed upward, first developing physically, then emotionally and socially, then mentally and cognitively, and finally spiritually and morally. To lead rich, fulfilling lives, however, we must start from the top of the pyramid and move downward. We start by defining purpose, values, meaning, and Ultimate Mission (spiritual), then create a view of the world, a cognitive mind-set—our version of reality—that reflects those sacred values and beliefs (mental). Then we summon the emotions that serve that purpose and mission (emotional). Finally, we act in ways that reflect our deepest values and grand purpose, aligning our behavior with our mission (physical).

This process is active. You don't uncover your purpose; you *create* it out of your experiences, your passions, your life as you have come to know it.

Once you find, define, and refine your purpose for existence—or "Ultimate Mission," in the language we use in our training courses at the Institute—you massively improve your chance for achieving fulfillment, even happiness. Doing so breeds success, and more "achievement."

This is the exact opposite of the equations so many people chase: *Success breeds happiness.*

Primacy of Purpose Pyramid

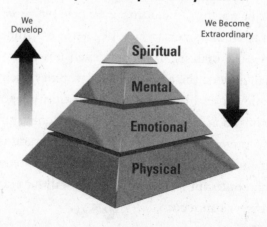

Wealth breeds happiness.
Perfection breeds happiness.
Prestige breeds happiness.
Buying that massive house will bring me happiness.
My next external achievement will bring me happiness.

They don't and they won't. Not only do these misguided pursuits disappoint in the long run; as I have written earlier, they all too often disappoint in the short run, as well.

When you find—or, more aptly, *choose*—your purpose, then you are the agent of your own happiness. You have the opportunity to harvest joy in both the pursuit *and* the achievement, the journey and the destination. With your purpose firmly in mind, these opportunities for happiness will actually come with relative ease. "Many persons have a wrong idea of what constitutes true happiness," wrote Helen Keller. "It is not attained through self-gratification but through fidelity to a worthy purpose." If you were deaf and blind from early childhood, like Helen Keller, what would it take for you to find happiness? How important would purpose be?

But what *is* purpose? More pointedly, what is *your* purpose? It is, first and last, something larger than yourself. Chris O., my colleague for many years, is a man with a purpose: As a boy, he developed an intense dislike of bullies. If he saw someone being taken advantage of, Chris would take on the bully—or five bullies. "Even if I had no chance," he once explained to me, "I still had a better chance than the kid being picked on." He learned to defend those who couldn't defend themselves, and eventually he became a champion boxer. He treated all those around him with fairness and respect because that was the opposite of what bullies do. He raised a family. Happily for him—and those around him—he discovered fairly early his "role in life," as he called it: "I saw myself as a sheepdog, preventing the wolves from getting to the sheep." Chris is just about the least combative, most at-peace, decent person I have ever met. Every breath he takes is purposeful. He is an extremely ethical and "successful" businessman. He's happy, too.

Narayanan Krishnan is a man with a purpose. As a chef at a fine hotel in Madurai, India, he came across a very old man eating his own waste to sate his hunger. Krishnan asked himself, "What is the purpose of my life? What am I going to do? In a star hotel, I feed all my guests—but in my hometown there are people going without food." He felt that the "ultimate purpose of life . . . is to give. Start giving. See the joy of giving." Which is what he now does for those in greatest need.

Jenette R. is a woman with a purpose. She is a thirty-eight-year-old with twenty years of service in the United States Army. As a lieutenant colonel, Jenette has been deployed three times to Iraq. Her last deployment was in combat service support of brigade nursing operations. She has no husband, no children, no close relatives, and both her parents died when she was still a teenager. "My family is the military," she told me. "And my combat service support team are my closest relatives." She went on to say, "I'm part of something that truly makes a difference in people's lives, and I'm very fulfilled by my work. I feel very fortunate to do what I do. I wake up every morning excited to make the lives of our soldiers a little better. I work very hard, but I'm more than willing to put in the extra effort. I feel very fortunate to do this work." And we are grateful for her service.

George Bailey, the beloved character played by Jimmy Stewart in the Christmas classic *It's a Wonderful Life*, is a man with a purpose—though he doesn't know it until it's starkly dramatized for him. He had *thought* his purpose was to become a world famous architect, create spectacular edifices, travel the globe, and shake the dust of his small town from his feet. But after he has the unique opportunity to see what life would have been like had he never been born, he understands what his true purpose always has been, and in fact it includes creating a thriving community as head of the family's modest building and loan association right there in his hometown. Rather than a world famous architect, he's an architect of other people's happiness.

Does purpose have to be "grand"? It must be larger than yourself and, just as importantly, particular to you. In my last book, *The Power of Story*, I wrote about a tennis player I worked with who was among the top 50 in the world. She had as much talent as anyone on tour but had lately become stuck—bad losses to lesser players, instances of choking. Even worse, her victories did not give her all that much pleasure. She dreaded the pain and agony she would experience from her next loss (which would last for days). Her coach and trainers became alarmed at her declining happiness.

When we first met, I asked her how she would define a successful life. I told her I wanted to know her real purpose behind everything she did, including playing professional tennis. She thought for a while and eventually came up with the following four things:

To be number one in the world.

To win Wimbledon.

To never worry financially.

To make enough money that I can buy whatever I want and travel wherever I want.

I then asked her if she wanted any of these on her tombstone. A grimace appeared immediately. She instantly knew they didn't belong there for her. I asked her why, and she said that they were too shallow and trivial. So I asked again about her purpose, her criteria for a successful life. I particularly wanted to know what would make her most proud if it were displayed on her tombstone. She thought for several moments and responded with a deep sigh, "I don't know." I told her to spend the evening thinking about it and give me her answer first thing in the morning.

When we met again, she was glowing. She'd thought very hard about the question and felt completely confident with her answer. "I want to be sunshine for all the people I care about and all the people who watch me play," she told me. "When they see me play, I want them to feel joy." I instantly knew she had come to something immensely important for her and we could now move forward in our work together. She had begun the hard work of creating what we call her "Ultimate Mission."

In the days and weeks that followed, she brought this newfound purpose to her training. She understood and believed in practice because she knew that it would help her become the best on-court presence she could be. Her competitive play was infused once again with passion, and for the fans who came to watch her she was cheerful in both victory and defeat. In the fiercest moments of competition, you could feel she was true to her goal, that she was "sunshine" for everyone. We all felt it.

Did she win? Yes, not Wimbledon, but something much better, something that would be found not in a trophy, but in the crowds she entertained. She had a few big wins over players ranked above her, stopped losing as much to less talented players, and cracked the top 20 in the rankings.

By re-purposing her tennis to bring joy into the lives of others and by not allowing any mistakes, bad luck, or missed opportunities during play to derail her, she created a transformation. If her tennis was to ignite a spark in others, then she first had to ignite it in herself in a genuine way. No head hanging, no expressions of defeat or dejection. She was now operating with a new scorecard and a new understanding of winning.

HOW DO YOU CLARIFY your purpose, your Ultimate Mission? And how will you know if it has the power to sustain you through calm seas and rough ones? So many people we work with don't know their purpose—or have picked the wrong one. How do you know if you have yours right?

In our executive courses, we ask participants to write down what they believe is their Ultimate Mission. To figure this out, these are the five most important questions they must ask themselves:

- What kind of person did I want to be when I grew up?
- What is something that I would be proud to accomplish and that doesn't have a shelf life or expiration date?

- Would that accomplishment improve my well-being and/or the well-being of others?
- Which character strengths would I like to develop in my life?
- What would I like to do with the strengths I develop? Will these capacities be in the service of myself or others?

Once you have a clearly defined purpose, it becomes your divining rod for targeting the specific character muscles you would like to grow. Sure, you can become a great tennis player—but toward what end? What do you use being a great tennis player *for*? To make so much money that you can buy your dream home and live happily ever after? To enjoy celebrity status (if in fact it's enjoyable)? Or do you use your greatness for something else? For the great Belgian champion Kim Clijsters, not only her success on the tennis court but also the energy she devotes to it are very much rooted in something else. "Whatever the obstacles, [her success] has a deeper meaning, a connection that goes back to her deceased father," writes Richard Eaton in *TennisLife* magazine. " 'My sister [Elke] and I, we miss him,' Clijsters says. 'We wish he was still here with us. Though we can't see him physically, we really feel like he's part of everything we do.' "

If you grow the "muscle" for compassion and the "muscle" for generosity (the how is discussed in detail in Chapter 5), what are you going to do with these strengths? Are these necessary to grow if you are to become a great asset for your future family and community? If you become a role model, then what would you like to model? Do you want to do something remarkable in the service of others? If so, what?

Questions like these are useful in getting clients to think about why they would spend their energy developing themselves into women or men of unique character. No matter how many times I've witnessed the transformation, it's amazing for me to see: Kids in our junior tennis program have gone through this exercise and refined their purpose from "I play tennis so I can get a college scholarship" to "I play tennis because I want to be known as a patient and calm person, I'm using tennis to help me get there, and the ups and downs of tennis give me lots of opportunities to practice" (Terry, age thirteen); or it goes from "I play tennis to become top 10 in my age bracket nationally" to "My success in tennis does not depend on the outcome of a match but the energy I put into the match; Tennis helps me improve my energy, eat healthier, try harder, and work on becoming the kind of person I want to be; I use tennis to help me stay disciplined when times are tough and help me reach my goal to be a doctor" (Ned, age eleven). And the sixteen- and seventeen-year-olds? The purpose statements they craft all on their own are astonishing. Indeed, kids and teenagers often get this exercise more easily than many of the fifty-something-year-old corporate executives we see.

Dan Jansen, Olympic gold medalist speed skater, describes an athlete's ultimate purpose with elegant simplicity: "If you use your sport to make you a better person, then you've won."

Peter

Peter, a forty-eight-year old partner in a mid-sized accounting firm, is a classic example of someone who had been using a scorecard that was not aligned with who he really wanted to be as a leader and father. Peter approached me during a break in one of our executive courses at the Institute. He wanted to share his story privately. "I'm just like my father," he told me. "He was a tough guy with me and I'm a tough guy with my kids. I had a terrible night last night, and it all started with the homework assignment you gave us. When I contemplated who I really wanted to be as a leader and a father at home with my children, I clearly did not want to be like my father. He never seemed to care about me, only my achievements. The only time I would get any recognition, attention, or approval from him was when I achieved something special—If I got all A's and one B, he would want to know why I got the B; if I played great the entire game but had one screwup, he would focus on the screwup. And I craved his affection. I chased every achievement I could, but I never felt good enough for him. I always felt that I fell short of his mark of the son he really wanted. He was a good man, but I felt I was not good enough for him. What's really crazy is that my father is seventy-one years old now and I'm still chasing achievements trying to win his approval and love.

"The thing that caused me so much agony last night was the realization that I'm doing the same thing with my children. I'm not as demanding as my father, but I'm clearly obsessed with my kids' achievements. I fear that they feel as I did—and still do—that they're loved for their achievements rather than for who they really are." Peter spent the remainder of the course building a new scorecard.

EACH PERSON HAS HIS or her own particulars that drive his or her unique Ultimate Mission. Some things, however, are universal. To figure out your mission, it is helpful to look at the truly universal concepts that characterize any enduring purpose. And to do that, it's useful to understand a bit about what the research community has unlocked over the past few decades. This dramatic knowledge will, I believe, help to define a new paradigm—a new scorecard. With this new scorecard, external achievement represents something much more profound, a meaningful weigh station on an equally endlessly fulfilling road. Understanding and embracing these new ideas—and others, on which I will elaborate—will enable us to live lives that are not just more meaningful, but more joyful and (dare I use the word?) successful, as well.

Children often say, "I didn't do that *on purpose*." But what if everything we did *was* "on purpose"—how fulfilling would our lives be then?

A SHORT HISTORY OF HAPPINESS RESEARCH

If you're interested in the "science of happiness," as it's sometimes, if simplistically, called, then this is your time. We're living through a

Golden Age. Great strides have been made in our understanding of well-being. It's no wonder: Well-being, fulfillment, happiness—name your paradise—is something everyone wants, yet so many of us are plagued by its elusiveness. It's no surprise that so many great minds have devoted themselves to trying to unlock its mysteries.

The upheavals in the study of happiness, achievement, motivation, and psychological needs have come in many forms. As I wrote earlier, over the last several years, there have been many studies that added substantially to our understanding. But the foundations for this understanding have been around for decades. For example, Self-Determination Theory* was introduced many years ago but has only recently begun to be applied to a world in which I've been involved for years—competitive sports coaching and training—where it has upended much of the existing dogma. Abraham Maslow's "hierarchy of needs" was first proposed nearly seventy years ago, but that famous pyramid (to which HPI's pays homage) has new relevance right now.

Among some of the essential contributors to this field of study:

- Neuroscientists, such as Joseph LeDoux, Michael Merzenich, Norman Doidge, and John Medina, for their study particularly of the prefrontal cortex—the brain region thought to be involved in, among other functions, personality expression and behavior moderation—and of the limbic system—whose structures are involved in functions including emotion and behavior. Especially notable are the *amygdala*, which is active in monitoring stimuli that "reward," and the *dentate gyrus*, implicated in the regulation of happiness. These scientists have made great advances in our understanding of how the brain is stimulated and how it regulates emotion, behavior, and, yes, even happiness.

---

* Self-Determination Theory (SDT) is a theory of human motivation that focuses on the degree to which behavior is self-initiated and self-motivated.

- Carol Dweck, for her tremendously important work on intelligence and "mind-set," and how those of different mind-sets take dramatically different approaches to challenge, performance, "failure," and growth. Dweck has had a profound effect on any researcher investigating the question of what it means to live a fulfilling and "successful" life.
- Roy Baumeister, for his work on belongingness and particularly on self-esteem—the importance of which, in its currently accepted definition, he considers overstated.
- The late Viktor Frankl, noted psychiatrist and Holocaust survivor, for his work on how we create meaning out of whatever we are exposed to. When one experiences obstacles or utter chaos, what things of value can be found? No matter how awful the environment, what can one focus on that will solidify a sense of purpose (if not happiness)?
- Ed Diener and Robert Biswas-Diener, whose brilliant work presents scientific evidence that happiness is not overrated.
- Robert Emmons, for devoting nearly his entire career to the scientific exploration of human gratitude.
- Barbara Fredrickson, for numerous contributions to the positive psychology movement—e.g., the evolutionary basis of positivity, her Broaden and Build positivity model, positivity ratios.

There are many other contributors, of course, quite a few of whom I reference in the endnotes and bibliography. There are also the writers and psychologists who have been helpful in translating some of the scientific and academic concepts, producing useful, compelling books for the general population—*Drive* by Daniel Pink, *The Talent Code* by Daniel Coyle, *Thrive* by Dan Buettner, and *The Self-Esteem Trap* by Polly Young-Eisendrath, to name just a few.

Briefly, I wish to pay particular attention to three men—Edward L. Deci and Richard M. Ryan, and then Martin E. P. Seligman—whose critically important work has provided the building blocks for solid science; whose contributions build on one another; and whose work I build on in this book.

Self-Determination Theory (SDT)

This groundbreaking theory, the brainchild of Deci and Ryan, has been around for more than three decades, but its significance has continually grown in applicability and stature as people in different fields understand its tenets. SDT really has two main components (at least as it applies to this book). The first pertains to extrinsic versus intrinsic motivation; the second, to the three major sustainable sources of motivation, which are:

- autonomy (I want to decide what to do with my life)
- mastery (I want to be really good at something for its own sake)
- relatedness (I want to make a difference in the world, leave a legacy for others)

Other research has confirmed the soundness of SDT—that these three, big innate needs, when met, provide us with the "nourishment" we need for optimal functioning and personal growth.

Motivation

In *The Handbook of Self-Determination,* Robert J. Vallerand defines extrinsic motivation as "behaviors performed to attain contingent outcomes" and intrinsic motivation as "behaviors performed out of interest and enjoyment." Extrinsic motivation, as has already been pointed out, drives one to engage in something to achieve a desired outcome separate from the activity. It leads one to engage out of obligation—to avoid feeling shame, for example. Most bluntly, it leads one to engage at less than optimal effectiveness. As Deci says in Daniel Pink's book *Drive,* where he recalls the explosive results his research yielded in experiments that tested the level of effectiveness of monetary rewards on worker productivity: "Nobody was expecting rewards would have a negative effect."

Whose goals are you pursuing: Your employer's? Your parents'? Your peer group's?

Or yours? Intrinsic motivation is the drive to engage in an activity for the pleasure and satisfaction inherent in the activity—e.g., to explore and understand new things, to try to surpass one's self, to experience the joy stimulated by the act of doing that thing. The three most powerful intrinsic sources of motivation? Autonomy, mastery, and relatedness.

Autonomy

The three basic needs, as Deci and Ryan saw them, became clear as they developed their ideas about extrinsic and intrinsic motivation. That is, the two big concepts are interwoven. Take autonomy: Our psychological need to feel that our behavior is self-initiated and self-endorsed is unsurprising; it's one of the keys to intrinsic motivation. Intrinsic goals are self-chosen because they are inherently satisfying to pursue.

People express their autonomy need in statements like "I want to be in charge of my life" and "I want to decide the life I want to live." They are happier and more satisfied with their lives *when the goals they are pursuing are their own*. When this need is met, researchers have confirmed better performance, more persistence, greater drive, and improved levels of psychological well-being.

Autonomy is such a profound need that no matter what state we are in, we crave it. Those who are destined to live a shortened life—as was Eugene O'Kelly, the CEO and chairman of KPMG who found out at age fifty-three that he had inoperable brain cancer—will still do everything in their limited time to fulfill this need. In Gene's case, he chose how he was best going to live out his last months, which he chronicled in his memoir, *Chasing Daylight*. Determining how he wanted to live in his remaining days and then aligning with those wishes deeply fulfilled his need for autonomy.

Fulfilling the need for autonomy does not mean that one must be independent of others.

Mastery

The second essential psychological need, as determined by SDT, is mastery. We must feel competent at what we do, and an important part of our identity is our sense that we can do things well that are important to us. We take great joy in learning, growing, and developing mastery. That we can improve and grow powerfully contributes to feelings of self-worth, and when we meet this need, we achieve richer, deeper lives.

When these first two needs are satisfied together, good things tend to happen: "Goals that people set for themselves and that are devoted to attaining mastery are usually healthy," writes Pink. "But goals imposed by others—sales targets, quarterly returns, standardized test scores, and so on—can sometimes have dangerous side effects."

Relatedness

We want to connect with others, and this third need, relatedness, is a human drive. When met, it satisfies our craving to be connected to and experience caring for others. We need to belong, to attach, to feel intimacy. You might be thinking, "Hey, wait a minute. Aren't autonomy and relatedness complete opposites?" Though it may seem so at first, it is not the case. Autonomy simply means that we must be able to choose how we extend our caring beyond ourselves. The human need to connect to and experience caring for others is so pervasive that when it is not met, healthy psychological functioning is seriously threatened. Baumeister and Leary, as well as others, have confirmed that when one acts in the service of others in ways that extend beyond self-interest, one's sense of personal esteem is powerfully affirmed.

"None of us can be truly human in isolation," writes Harold Kushner. "The qualities that make us human emerge only in the ways we relate to other people." Kushner also writes, "One human being is no human being"—an homage to the anthropological statement that "one chimpanzee is no chimpanzee." We do not—cannot—become human in isolation. Plato's "cave man" turned away from the light and had a degraded sense of humanity. Living in the shadows is not living.

. . . .

RELATING HPI's PYRAMID MODEL of character development to Deci and Ryan's three needs might be instructive here. As depicted in the following graphic, meeting the need for relatedness, which is referred to as a spiritual need in our model at HPI, is the highest priority in terms of personal fulfillment and happiness. Autonomy is a mental need and is second in terms of priority. Mastery is an emotional need and is third. The need for relatedness is met through the development of moral strengths of character, while needs for autonomy and mastery are met through the development of performance strengths of character. The key point in the graphic is the primacy of spiritual needs, specifically *relatedness*, in achieving a life of deep personal fulfillment.

One of the key components of purpose is a connection to something larger, something outside oneself. Charles Handy, the philosopher of management and organizational behavior, said, "True fulfillment is, I believe, vicarious. We get our deepest satisfaction from the fulfillment and growth and happiness of others."

Character Development and Need Fulfillment

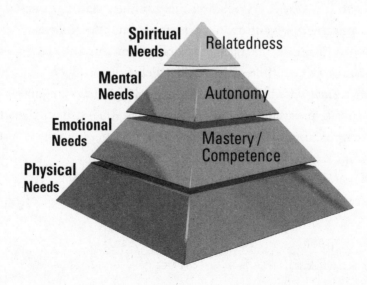

Tenzin Gyatso, the fourteenth Dalai Lama, may have captured best the nexus where all three SDT needs come together: "If you want others to be happy, practice compassion. If you want to be happy, practice compassion."

If you [autonomy] *want to be happy, practice* [mastery] *compassion* [relatedness].

How succinct.

Then again, maybe Aristotle said it more succinctly: "Happiness is the reward for virtue."

Positive Psychology

Martin Seligman, who first came to prominence with the theory of "learned helplessness,"* founded the movement known as "positive psychology" and has helped to reorient the way we look at human functioning. Instead of the model that for so long has prevailed, in which the goal is the eradication and treatment of dysfunction and unhappiness, the focus has shifted to nurturing positive human functioning. It's no longer about minimizing deprivation and more about maximizing thriving—or, to use Seligman's catchphrase, "flourishing." Taking direct aim at the *Diagnostic and Statistical Manual of Mental Disorders (DSM)*—the official reference produced by the American Psychiatric Association that not only classifies mental disorders and their prevention and treatment but also embeds a certain bottom-up way of thinking in doctors, patients, and the lay public—Seligman and coauthor Christopher Peterson produced, in 2004, *Character Strengths and Virtues (CSV)*, a volume that categorizes two dozen positive psychological characteristics. Included in the guide are strengths of wisdom and knowledge, courage, humanity, justice, temperance, and transcendence.

The shift from deficiency to strength is actually tectonic. The study of psychology was long rooted in a disease model of human

---

* "Learned helplessness" is a view that mental illness such as clinical depression may result from the perception that one has little or no control over the outcome of a situation.

nature. Historically, the focus for both researchers and practitioners had been to understand psychological illness, not psychological health; the *DSM* (along with the *International Classification of Diseases* [*ICD*] from the World Health Organization) helped to inculcate that way of thinking. In response, the *CSV*, and the larger positive psychology movement, chose to ask, *How do we thrive?* not *How do we get sick?* It asked, *How is a positive life possible? What is the best possible life we can live, and how?* Increasingly, the research community is exploring what's right about people rather than what's wrong. When you formulate the questions so differently, your answers and approach are bound to be different.

Extrapolating from a significant number of studies (he has been generous in bringing together the most important current research on well-being aside from his own), Seligman has concluded that there are five basic factors that contribute to thriving and well-being:

1. positive emotions (the most important of which is optimism, so that setbacks are perceived to be temporary)
2. engagement
3. positive relationships
4. meaning (connecting one's life to a purpose bigger than oneself)
5. accomplishment (mastery/competence)

Not only do we possess positive emotions (to take just one of the factors), but our capacity for them ought to be grown. Seligman refers to "signature strengths": Think of something you don't like about yourself, then use your signature strengths to get through it and be successful.

Seligman argues—as I have—that character contributes to and strengthens all five of his "well-being factors." The more you pursue positive character traits and values, the more you align yourself with factors that drive true happiness and well-being. Years of work and experience at HPI have driven home a simple but powerful understanding: Happiness without character is soft!

4

Character Comes in Two Types

You can easily judge the character of a man by how he treats
those who can do nothing for him.
—GOETHE

The word "character" derives from the Greek *charakter*, meaning "enduring or indelible mark." The philosopher Heraclitus proclaimed that "character is destiny."

Character isn't something we express just to appear good or because it's convenient. We live and grow character because we want to be happy. In fact, I firmly believe that how we engage and forge character has a direct relationship with our happiness.

But not all character is created equal.

Example: We push our children to get good grades, to have a positive attitude, to learn how to focus, to give their best effort in all things, to develop self-control, to be courageous, to learn to be critical thinkers, and so on. All beneficial qualities. They are among the strengths of character that drive performance excellence.

They are, as discussed earlier, all *performance character strengths*.

But no matter how diligent, focused, or optimistic your child—no matter how many performance character strengths he or she has mastered—if his or her *ethical/moral*★ *character strengths* are not firmly in place by adulthood, then the performance traits really don't matter nearly as much as far as genuine life "success."

How can that be? Performance character strengths clearly enhance success on society's scorecard. Moral character strengths, meanwhile, don't boast that kind of power, and they often obstruct these sorts of achievements. The fact is, they are very different types of capacities. In their fine work, *Smart and Good High Schools*, education professors and developmental psychologists Thomas Lickona and Matthew Davidson clearly make the distinction between moral and performance character. I would expand on their model in two crucial ways:

- As stated in Chapter 2, moral character strengths define the values that govern our relationship with others, while performance character strengths pertain to the values that govern our relationship with ourselves (and thus drive excellence and mastery).
- While I agree with Lickona and Davidson that the two types of character strengths are fully supportive of each other, I do not see them as equivalent. To me, there is a clear hierarchy: Moral character strengths trump performance character strengths every time.

For example, because their numbers greatly exceed expectations, a sales manager may give a free pass to members of his or her sales team when breaches of moral character surface. Indeed, when competitive pressures are intense and there's a crunch to make numbers, managers often look the other way, and priorities like respect for others, honesty, fairness, and loyalty take a backseat.

As long as managers witness their team members advancing in the performance character sphere—through gains in team confidence, perseverance, focus, resiliency, positivity, and mental toughness—

★ Ethical and moral are used interchangeably.

they feel good about their mentoring and leadership. And they should. But, as history so often painfully reveals, the most important responsibility of leadership resides not in the performance sphere of character, but in the ethical. The greatest return by leaders will, over time, come in their mentoring of moral strengths.

Consider this: Bernie Madoff. Core leaders at WorldCom, Enron, Adelphia, Arthur Andersen, the Nixon White House, etc. What did they all have in common? Yes, of course: They all suffered from a decided lack of moral character. But what else?

Most of them—I'd wager pretty much all of them—possessed an impressive list of individual performance character strengths. Perseverance. Focus. Resiliency. Self-discipline. Commitment. Optimism. Creativity. You can't achieve mastery and excellence without these traits. Tiger Woods had—has—an array of performance character strengths that are hard to match. So, too, for Michael Vick, Pete Rose, Barry Bonds, Floyd Landis, Mike Tyson, and on and on.

Indeed, here's a more comprehensive list of *performance character strengths*: willingness to invest effort, perseverance, self-discipline, constructiveness, capacity for hard work, optimism, determination, wisdom, positive attitude, hope, love of learning, creativity, ability to think critically, humor, confidence, focus, commitment, openness to challenge, resiliency, self-control, ambition, adaptability, resourcefulness, reliability, competitiveness, responsibility, punctuality, decisiveness, mental toughness, bravery, self-compassion, patience with self.

Not too shabby.

Now here's a list of *moral character strengths*: capacity for love, caring, kindness, honesty, truthfulness, integrity, humility, gratitude, fairness, generosity, compassion, loyalty, patience, respect for others, sense of honor, sense of duty.

Pretty impressive, as well.

Upon reflection, though, one comes to see that they are not, in fact, equal.

- Which character strengths, performance or moral, have the highest value in terms of your Ultimate Mission?
- Which character strengths, moral or performance, do you most want your employees or team members to embody?
- Would you still admire someone who possessed nearly all the moral character strengths but few performance character strengths?
- Would you still admire someone who possessed nearly all of the performance character strengths but few moral character strengths?
- Can one possess great performance character strengths that enable one to dominate in one's field of specialty—e.g., medicine, law, sports—and possess few moral character strengths?
- What are the character strengths you most want embodied by the following people: your boss, your spouse, your family members?
- Which consistently receive your highest priority, moral strengths or performance strengths?

Keeping your answers to these questions in mind, choose the top six character strengths you most want for your life, either moral or performance, from the following lists and rank them from 1 to 6.

MY TOP SIX CHARACTER STRENGTHS

1. _____
2. _____
3. _____
4. _____
5. _____
6. _____

From which category are your top six drawn, moral or performance?

PERFORMANCE CHARACTER STRENGTHS

Effort Investment	Hope	Seeking Challenges	Competitiveness
Perseverance	Love of Learning	Resiliency	Responsibility
Self-Discipline	Creativity	Self-Control	Punctuality
Constructiveness	Critical Thinking	Ambition	Decisiveness
Capacity for Hard Work	Humor	Adaptability	Mental Toughness
Optimism	Confidence	Resourcefulness	Bravery
Determination	Focus	Reliability	Self-Compassion
Concentration	Best Energy Investment	Courage	Patience with Self
Wisdom	Commitment	Positivity	Diligence

MORAL CHARACTER STRENGTHS

Love for Others	Truthfulness	Justice	Loyalty to Others
Care for Others	Integrity	Fairness	Patience with Others
Kindness	Humility	Generosity	Respect for Others
Honesty	Gratefulness	Compassion	Honor

Remember, performance character strengths are values that govern our relationship with *ourselves*. Moral character strengths are values that govern our relationship with *others*. To do well on society's scorecard, you'll need to be in possession of a whole host of performance character strengths. *To truly succeed* as a human being, however, moral strengths of character are mandatory. As Lickona and Davidson conclude in *Smart & Good High Schools*, "Whereas moral virtues are intrinsically good, performance virtues can be used for bad ends."

When I was a young boy, one of my action heroes was Marshal Matt Dillon, the central character in the long-running TV western series *Gunsmoke*. It was Dillon's fast gun, his fearless attitude, and unfailing courage in the face of impossible odds that captured my imagination. Years later, as an adult, however, I came to realize that the most captivating element of the show for me was the *moral* character of Matt Dillon and, to a lesser extent, of Kitty, owner and operator of the Long Branch Saloon; of Chester and Festus, Dillon's quirky but always trustworthy deputies; and of Doc Adams, Dodge City's only doctor. I appreciated most that at the core of every show was a moral dilemma that had to be resolved by one or more of the show's main characters. Even today, I enjoy watching *Gunsmoke* reruns and studying the moral reasoning process Matt Dillon uses to comply with his ever-present values and commitment to justice. In spite of Dodge City's incessant lawlessness and near-constant temptation to retreat to the dark side, Dillon always prevails. The show's appeal would have abruptly ceased, I am certain, were Dillon ever to have compromised his moral principles, in spite of his lightning-fast gun and undaunted courage.

This kind of moral strength and clarity are what we aspire to, even though we haven't always articulated it to ourselves. Superheroes who are less "real" than Marshal Matt Dillon can have all the performance character strengths in the world, but if they should lose one or more such power (confidence, patience, X-ray vision, etc.), we'll still root for them. However, if they suffer a lapse in their ethical /moral character, then their whole legacy is, to our eyes, seriously jeopardized. On the flip side, Darth Vader and most every other embodiment of evil can exhibit just as much performance character as any of those on the right side of moral law. But it is ultimately Darth Vader's bankruptcy of moral character traits that dooms him.

The pivotal event in the life of virtually every figure we love and admire deeply revolves around that character's ethical battles and challenges. Our heroes' moral character is what defines them, much as it will eventually define you. Rick, from *Casablanca*, giving away his letter of passage to Ilsa's Nazi-fighting husband; Eric Liddell, from *Chariots of Fire*, forgoing running an Olympic race held on a Sunday; Belle, from *Beauty and the Beast*, keeping her word and returning to the castle of the Beast, her captor, because that vow helped her to win

Importance of Moral vs. Performance Character

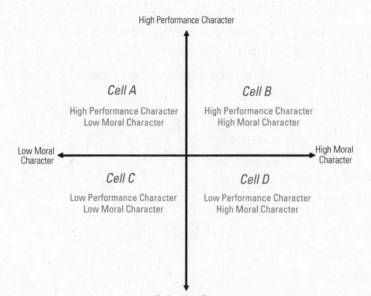

her father's release—everything that really matters about them has to do with their character, and most importantly, their ethical character.*

"CELLING" CHARACTER:
MORAL VERSUS PERFORMANCE

The moral/performance character matrix depicted above contains four cells: Cell A represents a person possessing high performance character but low moral character; Cell B, a person possessing high performance character as well as high moral character; Cell C, a person possessing both low performance and low moral character;

---

* Compared to movies, books tend to be more psychologically complex—at least those not written foremost for children and younger people. For every beloved character defined by his or her ethical character (or at least his or her attempt to be ethical)—e.g., Holden Caulfield in *The Catcher in the Rye*, Atticus Finch in *To Kill a Mockingbird*, Harry Potter—there are equally memorable characters defined by their troubled relationship to, or even absence of, ethical character—Jay Gatsby, Ahab, Humbert Humbert.

and, finally, Cell D, a person possessing low performance but high moral character.

By answering the following eleven questions, your understanding of and appreciation for the relative importance in your life of moral versus performance character strengths should crystallize.

1. Rank the four cells by who you most want to be in life.
a) Rank #1 Cell _____
b) Rank #2 Cell _____
c) Rank #3 Cell _____
d) Rank #4 Cell _____

2. Rank the four cells by who you most want to be as a business leader.
a) Rank #1 Cell _____
b) Rank #2 Cell _____
c) Rank #3 Cell _____
d) Rank #4 Cell _____

3. Rank the four cells by who you most want your employer/boss to be.
a) Rank #1 Cell _____
b) Rank #2 Cell _____
c) Rank #3 Cell _____
d) Rank #4 Cell _____

4. Rank the four cells by who you most want your children to be in life.
a) Rank #1 Cell _____
b) Rank #2 Cell _____
c) Rank #3 Cell _____
d) Rank #4 Cell _____

5. Rank the four cells by who you most want your spouse/partner to be in life.

a) Rank #1 Cell _____
b) Rank #2 Cell _____
c) Rank #3 Cell _____
d) Rank #4 Cell _____

6. As a leader, if you had to make a choice between low performance or low moral, which would you choose?
Cell _____

7. Which cell best describes how those who know you well perceive you as a leader?
Cell _____

8. List your 3 greatest moral strengths of character (see page 75):
a) _____
b) _____
c) _____

9. List your 3 greatest moral deficiencies of character (see page 75):
a) _____
b) _____
c) _____

10. List your 3 greatest performance strengths of character (see page 75):
a) _____
b) _____
c) _____

11. List your 3 greatest performance deficiencies of character (see page 75):
a) _____
b) _____
c) _____

Moral character guides not only one's treatment of and interactions with others, but ensures that one is ethical in the pursuit of extrinsic goals. In my view, to live a truly successful life, one may or may not have certain performance character strengths (certainly, you'll need *some*), but one must have a solid number of moral character strengths. These are not negotiable. The acquisition of moral character strengths, therefore, represents the apex of healthy human development.

Though this may seem clear, it is by no means easy. As David Brooks writes in *The Social Animal*, "the unconscious soulsphere is a coliseum of impulses vying for supremacy . . . Compassion and pity may emerge at the cost of fortitude, toughness, and strength. The virtue of courage and heroism may clash with the virtue of humility and acceptance. The cooperative virtues may clash with the competitive virtues."

Yet I maintain that moral character strengths represent the fundamental core of what it means to be a fully functional, healthy human being. And if that's so, business leaders should do everything they can to teach them. Rather than being obsessed by financial outcomes, managers should focus on the path employees take to achieve those outcomes. Ethical leadership should be granted preeminent status by corporate boards and all C-suite executives.

5

Building Your Scorecard and Training the Muscles of Character

As a single footstep will not make a path on the earth, so a
single thought will not make a pathway in the mind.
To make a deep physical path, we walk again and again.
To make a deep mental path, we must think over and over the
kind of thoughts we wish to dominate our lives.

—Henry David Thoreau

As I've noted, great new research and intriguing interpretations of past research about the subject of well-being have emerged in the last few years, giving us a clearer picture of what does and does not make us sustainably happy. The real issue now: How do you synthesize the most important insights and lessons and apply them to your own life and to those whose lives you shape? If you're going to create and follow a new scorecard, one that guides how you operate at work, organize your day, and relate to those most important to you—well, how exactly do you do that?

We bring the message contained within these pages into our training programs at the Institute. Most of our clients are businesspeople. We not only introduce these concepts, but we're expected to "solve" the most important problems that surface during the two-and-a-half-day course. The people who attend are typically highly successful from society's perspective, but many have some substantial dissatisfaction with their lives. Of the executives who come through the Institute:

- 32 percent believe they are not as competent as others think they are
- 27 percent are disappointed in themselves
- 40 percent see their lives as pragmatic and responsible, but joyless
- 24 percent feel their current life story is stagnant
- 15 percent report the dominant theme in their life is frustration
- 24 percent blame their job for most of their problems

Many of the people coming have "earned" A's and B's on society's scorecard but score C's, D's, and F's, with an occasional A or B, on very different, far less extrinsically oriented scorecards. Often these clients will confront the painful truth and then a mystified look overtakes them. *How could this have happened?* The disconnect between who they are now and who they want to be in terms of their most cherished values is disturbing and disruptive. *Why the hell did you have to bring this up on top of everything else I'm dealing with? I've got too much on my plate to deal with this now!*

Although this defensive reaction is normal and predictable, it also blocks any positive growth going forward. The noted psychologist Leon Festinger referred to the tension that occurs when a belief or value is challenged as cognitive dissonance. Festinger believed that human beings generally respond to the dissonance in two main ways. One is to dismiss the incongruence by deluding oneself that the conflict really doesn't matter or to discredit the source of the disturbing information altogether. The other is to distort the disruptive information in such a way that it no longer causes tension. These defensive reactions impede efforts to resolve discrepancy that might exist between one's core values and one's actual behavior. They serve to restore self-esteem without addressing the underlying cause of the discomfort.

So how can you prevent yourself from becoming defensive when the discrepancy between your values and your behavior is made so clear-cut? From our experience at the Institute, the best answer comes from Claude Steele, the social psychologist. According to his "self-affirmation theory," when people reflect on their most cherished values and attributes—their best self, so to speak—they tend to be more open-minded and willing to face challenging issues. Similarly, researcher Jennifer Crocker from the University of Michigan contends that "writing about important values enables people to transcend concerns about self-image or self-worth. Writing essays about important values reminds people what they care about beyond themselves, and may induce positive other-directed feelings." For close to two decades, this is precisely what we've done at the Institute.

A NEW SCORECARD

Have you heard any of these before?

Winning is everything.

Second best is for losers.

Win at all costs.

Show me a good loser and I'll show you a loser.

When it's all said and done, winning is what matters.

All these sentiments might describe the driving force behind Society's Scorecard, which, whether we're conscious of its existence or not, is an immensely powerful, even addictive, document—one we so want to "ace" that it can make us do things we don't really want to do:

- A CEO, a man of deep faith, looks the other way when his CFO fails to include sensitive data in his financial report to the board. The CEO knows this has been done to prevent panic and preserve shareholder equity. He believes that the omission was done for a noble cause.
- An HR director intentionally exaggerates the deficiencies of a potential job hire and by doing do improves her chances of getting the job herself.

- A highly ambitious employee uses information he received in confidence to gain a substantial competitive edge over members of his own team.

As it's now constructed, Society's Scorecard is concerned only with ends, not means. It focuses on results, not the process by which you achieve those results, or how that process may warp you. How are you doing on it?

While Society's Scorecard measures a very narrow, externally driven set of criteria, your *personal scorecard*, the one you're going to create, fine-tune, and reference often, need not be a document that taunts, stresses, and enervates you every time you think of it. Rather, because it will be a document that measures who you are becoming as a consequence of the energy you invest in meaningful activities, creating and maintaining it can be invigorating, heartening, confirming.

To compare not only the grades one might earn on these two very different scorecards but also the feelings evoked by filling out the two scorecards, let's take Karl as an example.

At the time of his visit to the Human Performance Institute, Karl was fifty-two years old and married with two children, ages nine and twelve. He was in the midst of an agonizing divorce. According to Karl, his parents instilled in him a strong work ethic and commitment to make whatever sacrifices were necessary to meet or exceed expectations. In crafting what we at HPI call the "Old Story," Karl wrote, "I was conditioned to 'Do what you're told and never be satisfied with second best.'" Karl's résumé was filled with honors, awards, and other extraordinary achievements. He had been high school valedictorian and captain of the football team, and his classmates voted him "Most Likely to Succeed." He'd graduated from Princeton with a 3.8 GPA, then earned an MBA from NYU in finance. Karl passed all three exams to become a certified financial analyst in record time. Three years ago he had been appointed CFO of a large multinational public corporation. With salary and bonuses, his income was in the seven figures.

After many hours of doggedly facing the truth, Karl described himself in the following way:

I'm a conformer, the good soldier who always did what he was told, who became whatever was necessary to be success-ful. In a sense, I've learned to become a world-class chame-leon, learned how to morph myself into being whatever was needed to jump past every obstacle placed before me. . . . I'm addicted to achievement. I'm never satisfied with my accom-plishments. I always push for more. No matter what I do, it never seems enough to bring me happiness. . . . Even though I know I have achieved a lot, I have a persistent feeling of emp-tiness inside. I keep hoping that my next achievement will bring me the inner peace and sense of personal value that I am longing for.

When Karl was asked to ponder questions such as "What legacy do you want to leave behind?"; "What matters most to you?"; "What are your deepest values?"; and "What makes your life really worth living?" he became very uncomfortable and, in his own words, "quite emotional and confused." Karl went on to say,

I can't remember the last time I cried, but I cried last night— a lot. Feelings of sadness, guilt, and failure completely con-sumed me. I faced the truth that I didn't know myself very well. I've never learned to really think about who I truly want to be as opposed to what others want me to be. . . . All I ever wanted was for others to value me. Most importantly, I wanted that from my parents. My answer was simply to be the best at everything. I just assumed that if I achieved great things, I'd be a great success in life. And happy.

After writing his story, I asked Karl to grade himself on Society's Scorecard:

Fame (how well known you are)	A-
Money (how much money you have)	A
Power (how many people you control)	A
Materialism (how much stuff you have)	A+
Beauty	
(how much effort and money you invest	
in being handsome and attractive)	B
Status/Position (prestige of your title)	A

Karl spent many hours constructing his own personal scorecard and gave himself a very different GPA:

Positivity	C
Kindness	D
Humility	C
Compassion	C-
Gratefulness	D
Patience	D
Selfless Love of Others (mostly family)	C-
Engagement with Family	C-

As of this writing, Karl is constructing a new identity, one that he has chosen and that is clearly within his sphere of control—one that can never be stolen from him. He definitely has a long way to go, but according to him, a monumental shift has occurred in how he approaches everything. In his own words, "The softer side of me is emerging and the positive feedback I'm getting from others confirms the changes I feel on the inside are working their way to the outside."

According to Karl, his new scorecard is both liberating and exciting.

BUILDING AND LIVING YOUR SCORECARD

The process of constructing a new life scorecard begins by writing out answers to the following questions:

- What legacy do you want to leave behind?
  How do you want to be remembered?
- How do you want people to describe you?
- Who do you want to be in life—who is your best self?
- Who and what matters most to you?
- What are your deepest values?
- How would you define true success for your life?
- What makes your life really worth living?

Answers to these questions form the core of what will eventually become the single most important document in your life: your Ultimate Mission. From your most cherished values, from the people you love and care most about, from life as it has been handed down to you, from all of your life experiences—what is your most important mission in life? Your answer becomes the cornerstone of your new scorecard and your definitive moral stake in the ground. Here are just a few sample Ultimate Mission statements. The first is my own and the next three are from clients:

> In all decisions and choices, I consider the welfare of my family first and foremost. My life and behavior reflect a constant commitment to the highest ethical standards. I treat others with dignity, respect, and compassion. I fully acknowledge that energy is my most precious resource. In keeping with this, I work daily to achieve the highest level of spiritual, mental, emotional, and physical fitness in my life. I commit to bringing passion, positive energy, and hope to life's challenges. I work courageously to make a lasting difference, not to play it safe or take the easy road. I am both grateful for and generous with what I have. I will never surrender my spirit.—*Jim Loehr*

> I want to be remembered as a loving and caring mother to my two children and wife to my husband, someone who brought joy, happiness, and hope to all she touched. I want my life to

be a living testimony to my most cherished beliefs and values. I want others to know what I stand for by the way I live my life. I want to be remembered as a great teacher, filled with patience and kindness, whose love of learning was contagious to all.—*Jan B.*

What I want most is for my life to be a testament to courage; courage first to follow my Christian beliefs and be a devoted follower of Christ's word; courage to be the father and husband my parents were for me and my father was for my mother; courage to show gratitude and forgiveness in life's most difficult moments; courage to put the welfare of others before myself—always. In both good times and bad, I want to be remembered for courageously taking the road less traveled for one reason—it was the right thing to do.—*Dan K.*

I want most importantly to be remembered as a person of great character, unwilling to compromise for material gains. I want to be remembered as a person of compassion for others, integrity, and strong moral fiber. I want these to be the most treasured gifts I leave behind for my children.—*Maria M.*

Once you've crafted your Ultimate Mission to your satisfaction (it will never be complete and will be continually evolving and deepening over time), you are now ready to use it in the construction of your character scorecard. Prioritize the character strengths represented or implied in your Ultimate Mission and rank them beginning with the most important and progressing downward to least important. Your list should contain eight to ten character strengths, half or more of which should be moral.

Here are a couple of lists derived from the Ultimate Mission statements just provided:

Jim Loehr: Loving/Kind, Having Integrity, Respecting Others, Compassionate, Grateful, Hopeful, Courageous, Generous, Positive, Determined

Jan B.: Trustful, Loving/Kind, Having Integrity, Hopeful, Inspirational, Patient, Positive, Respectful, Fair, Honorable

Once you've completed your highest priority character list, take five to ten minutes and write about "your best self." This self-affirming exercise is to prevent resistance and defensiveness should your grades be embarrassingly low: In most cases, serious deficiencies are revealed. In the "your best self" exercise, you should simply describe the things you are most proud of about yourself. Discuss the character strengths and traits that you believe represent your greatest assets as a person at the current time. You can describe both moral and performance character strengths.

After completing the "your best self" writing exercise, grade yourself on each of the character strengths in your list using the following grading system:

A—Outstanding
B—Good
C—Okay
D—Poor
F—Failure

The grade you give yourself should reflect two things: (1) the relative strength of your character muscles* as they are today and (2) the quantity, quality, focus, and intensity of energy you currently invest in that particular character muscle (more on that later in this chapter).

---

* Strengths of character such as integrity, kindness, or positivity are analogous to bicep or hamstring strength. Character strength is built in the same way physical strength is built—focused repetition of energy investment.

Review your list one more time. Decide which character strengths you most want and need to grow at this time in your life. Pay special attention to those strengths that received poor grades. Select your top five to start working on and rank them in order of importance to you.

All that remains now is to select which character trait you want to grow first and then develop a concrete plan on how you will make training investments over the next fourteen days.

Once you've completed the two weeks of training, select another character trait for the next two weeks. After all your top priorities are completed, start again with the same list or create a new one, whichever you feel will help you the most. Use the examples below to get you started, and refer to pages 93–95 for a summary of all the steps.

STEP 1

SAMPLE ULTIMATE MISSION

In all decisions and choices, I consider the welfare of my family first and foremost. My life and behavior reflect a constant commitment to the highest ethical standards. I treat others with dignity, respect, and compassion. I fully acknowledge that energy is my most precious resource. In keeping with this, I work daily to achieve the highest level of spiritual, mental, emotional, and physical fitness in my life. I commit to bringing passion, positive energy, and hope to life's challenges. I work courageously to make a lasting difference, not to play it safe or take the easy road. I am both grateful for and generous with what I have. I will never surrender my spirit.

STEP 2

SAMPLE BEST SELF EXERCISE

When I'm at my best, when I am most proud of who I am, I'm positive with others and myself, I'm loving and kind, most importantly to my family members and colleagues at work. I also feel good about myself when I feel compassion and empathy for those less fortunate than I. I can get so preoccupied with my own needs and ambitions. The fact is I have so much to be thankful for. When I feel grateful for what I have, I like who I am. I also like myself best when I'm generous, hopeful, and show the courage and determination to follow my convictions.

TOP 10 CHARACTER STRENGTHS EXAMPLE

STEPS 3–5

CHARACTER STRENGTHS	GRADE	PRIORITY
1. Loving/Kind	C+	# 2
2. Integrity	A–	# 6
3. Respect for Others	B+	# 8
4. Compassion	B–	# 3
5. Gratitude	B	# 1
6. Optimistic/Hopeful	C+	# 4
7. Courageous	B–	# 9
8. Generous	B+	# 7
9. Positive	C	# 10
10. Determined	C+	# 5

GRADING SYSTEM

A—Outstanding B—Good C—Okay D—Poor F—Failure

The grade is based on the relative strength of the character traits as they are today and the quantity, quality, focus, and intensity of energy invested.

SAMPLE CHARACTER SCORECARD
(TOP 5 CHARACTER STRENGTHS TO GROW)

PRIORITY	CHARACTER STRENGTH LIST	GRADE
# 1	Gratitude	B
# 2	Loving/Kind	C+
# 3	Compassion	B−
# 4	Optimistic/Hopeful	C+
# 5	Determined	C+

STEPS 6–12

SAMPLE TRAINING LOG

FOR WEEKS OF FEBRUARY 1–7 AND 8–14

PRIORITY	CHARACTER STRENGTH*	GRADE
# 1	Gratitude	B

HOW TRAINED

Begin each day by listing five things for which you can be grateful for and write about them in a journal for a minimum of five minutes.

DATE	YES / NO	DATE	YES / NO
Feb 1	X	Feb 8	X
Feb 2	X	Feb 9	X
Feb 3	X**	Feb 10	X
Feb 4	X	Feb 11	X
Feb 5	X	Feb 12	X
Feb 6	X	Feb 13	X
Feb 7	X	Feb 14	X

* Remember, you are only to work on one character strength every two weeks. Working on more than one becomes overwhelming very quickly.

** A check in the No column simply means you failed to invest the required energy.

STEPS FOR BUILDING YOUR NEW CHARACTER SCORECARD

Step 1 Create your Ultimate Mission statement.

Step 2 Write about your "best self" for ten to fifteen minutes.

Step 3 Identify eight to ten character strengths (moral or performance) that are aligned with your Ultimate Mission and most represent who you want to be in life.

Step 4 Grade yourself (A to F) on each of the eight to ten character strengths you identified in Step 3.

Step 5 Prioritize your eight to ten character strengths from one to ten. Choose the top five character strengths you feel you most want and need to grow to achieve real success in life.

Step 6 Select the highest priority character strength you wish to target for growth for the next two weeks (e.g. gratitude, compassion, kindness, truthfulness, optimism, respect for others).

Step 7 Determine how you will make energy investments in the targeted character "muscle." Refer to pages 103–108 for specific strategies. For example, to build gratefulness, spend three minutes every morning for fourteen days writing a list of all the things you are grateful for. For kindness, do eight acts of kindness over the next fourteen days.

Step 8 Prepare a simple training log where you record every training deposit you make in the targeted character strength during the fourteen days (e.g., number of gratitude lists, acts of kindness).

Step 9 Put prompts and notes everywhere to remind you of your commitment to build the targeted character trait (e.g., put the word "positive" or "grateful" or "humble" on your bathroom mirror, screen saver, or smartphone).

Step 10 At the end of two weeks, select another character strength you wish to grow. Repeat steps 7, 8, and 9. If you choose, you may continue to repeat the training rituals you used to build previously targeted character "muscles," but your training efforts should be focused intensely on the new one to be strengthened.

Step 11 Once the first five character strengths that you targeted for growth have received the two weeks of training, prepare a new list of five and repeat the steps again. You can keep the same five or select new ones.

> **Step 12** Grade yourself every two weeks on your original eight- to ten-character-strength scorecard (Step 4). As you train, you will witness steady growth over time. Changes or additions to your scorecard can be made wherever you feel it right to do so.

Given that this is your new scorecard, it is vital that you be actively involved in its construction. While that should seem obvious, other influences—including society, parents, coaches, bosses, coworkers, and friends—often dictate your scorecard, which undermines your autonomy. Others can inform, encourage, even persuade you, sure—but you must be the architect of your own scorecard.

Though you define it, the scorecard will have at least one restriction: It must contain not just performance character strengths but moral as well (if you have any doubt, check page 75 in Chapter 4). I assure you that any scorecard that ignores moral/ethical strengths simply will not work. Without putting these moral imperatives front and center, you cannot become the extraordinary person you wish to be.

With this new character scorecard, it will be harder to know than it was with the previous scorecard if you're winning or losing. After all, how exactly does one measure respect for others? Quantifying "success," "achievements," and "victories" will not be as easy as it was when you were evaluating yourself against quarterly returns, expected salary, bonus size, the number of trophies or your ranking. Ironically, though, the previous scorecard was likely not written down, perhaps not even articulated. This scorecard *will* be written down and *will* be continually and explicitly articulated.

It's critical to understand that your new character scorecard does not shun achievement. It gives achievement and winning a new context, one in which they are a vehicle for something intrinsic and character-based. For example, if you have been accepted to an elite university—or any university, for that matter—then graduating from there may be one of many goals you "achieve." That said, the goal would not appear on your scorecard as, say, "graduate from Northwestern." Instead, the pursuit of the achievement of graduation will be used, first and last, to help make you more persistent, to increase your love of learning, or to deepen your gratitude, to name just a few possibilities. To be blunt, graduating from college actually has relatively little value in and of itself, a fact that is much harder to recognize with the old scorecard and practically heretical to say in certain polite company. However, a college degree can have tremendous value if you have developed both moral and performance character strengths in your pursuit of it.

I contend—and I have seen countless validating examples of this in my own work—that once you get the new scorecard going and really live it, you not only become a stronger, happier human being, but you are very likely to experience *more* victories and *more* external achievements, too. Why? Because you will be getting far more out of yourself than ever before. Happier, more fulfilled people constantly outperform those who are unhappy and dissatisfied. You will be happier than you were, and happiness, as discussed earlier, breeds success. We've seen how the reverse statement—success breeds happiness—is simply not true.

Kerry: Closing the gap between what I do and who I want to be

Kerry, a forty-two-year-old African-American woman, is vice president at a Midwestern insurance firm, with sixty-five direct reports. She grew up in Jackson, Mississippi, to—in her words—"post–civil rights" parents. "They really pushed education and winning in the white man's world," Kerry told me some time after taking our workshop, "and impressed on me the idea that if you get the right degrees and have the right mind-set, you can overcome all the structural barriers that society has set up. I really took that seriously and worked really hard to achieve very specific objectives." She went to Stanford, where she majored in engineering, then to Harvard Business School. "At the time it didn't hit me how much I calibrated my success on having gone to the best schools and taking the toughest major." After business school she was recruited by a top-tier management consulting firm and continued to "hit all those marks for what a success looks like."

Every part of her life was "an extension of that mind-set," she said. "You're supposed to get married? I got married. You're supposed to have two kids? I have two kids." She transitioned from getting degrees to landing enviable jobs to acquiring material things—and she also put her relationships in the "category of accomplishments."

Kerry eventually left the management consulting firm and, after some time off following the birth of her children, assumed her current position as a VP. The people who made up her new team were more diverse than any group she'd worked with before, and she found she wasn't particularly good at handling the different personalities. Perhaps not surprisingly, it was around this time that she realized that, in her words, "my skills in personal relationships were also relatively immature." She did not feel as if she had command over "those virtues" one needs to uphold at work and at home. Everything was coming to a head. At a certain point, she stopped to ask herself, "What am I doing this for? What kind of legacy do I want as mother and wife and leader?" "I couldn't play that 1950s game, where I'm one person at work and another person at home. I know that's crap because, really, who you are is who you are. It manifests itself wherever you are."

As you can see, before Kerry came through our workshop she was on the cusp of making some big changes. "I started questioning the things that were really the most important in my life and what wasn't. And the things that were—my family and my legacy—were honestly much more difficult and required a lot of training and thoughtful work. Those other, material accomplishments, hard as they seemed, were a lot easier. For the longest time, I looked only at external goals and, getting them, said, 'Here's who I really am' to the world. Meanwhile, living like that meant subordinating everything else that really mattered to me."

Kerry started to think, too, about how she approached her job. For a long time she had "looked at those on my team as units of production instead of real people. No more."

At HPI, she said, "my 'aha' moment was realizing that you can move from a more extrinsically driven scorecard to a more pro-foundly intrinsic one. Matching my energy investment with my most cherished values helped me a great deal. I realized how I gave the best of Kerry in my time at work, and when I came home, I was hungry, tired, and impatient. No one in the family was getting the very best Kerry. So I started to work hard at it. When I got in the garage after returning from work, I would take a measure of my energy level. I would ask myself, "What does it take to be sweet and patient and engaged when I walk through the door? How can I be my best self for my husband and my children? Does it mean turning off my BlackBerry now? Does it mean getting something to eat and drink as soon as I get in, so I'm not so ravenous that I'm distracted? Did it mean that, even though I was an NPR junkie, maybe I should have forgone listening to that on the way home and hearing more about the war in Libya, and listened to some soothing music in-stead?" Poignantly, Kerry, who's been married for thirteen years and has a ten-year-old daughter and eight-year-old son, described how she understood the urgency of the need to change. "If I'm grouchy when I walk through the door and that's how my kids experience me—well, what's that? In eight more years, my daughter will leave for college. Am I going to be more present for her then, when she's no longer around?"

At work, she made changes, too. "I'm my very best self in the early work hours, so I stopped doing email right when I got into the office, like I used to do. Instead, I moved my one-on-one meetings with direct reports to early in the morning. If I was really going to stop seeing my team as units of production anymore and start seeing them as people, then I needed to give them my best energy so I could be fully engaged. It's almost ridiculous what such a simple change can do."

This new focus on character produced even more changes. For the first time, Kerry could feel a real sense of purpose at work. "My human resources department meets with 'high-potential' leaders to talk about career development. In my most recent such discussion, rather than talking just about the next level to reach, or wanting more responsibility or more opportunity to drive results or more money, I shared my personal mission and talked about matching my next role to the specific things that I really want to establish as my legacy in the workplace. First, I want to model strengths of character such as integrity, humility, and gratefulness to the people who I am privileged to lead. Second, I want to have an impact on diversity in our company—not just as it applies to race, gender, or age, but also the diversity of thought. I see that as part of our core competitive strength.

"Now there's a higher purpose to what I do every day," says Kerry. "I hope I can close the gap between what I do and who I want to be." While she's found her purpose, she's also been working to improve some of her traits, including being "less aggressive and more assertive."

Once Kerry connected her grand purpose in life to work, she could begin using her work to leverage building strengths of character that created the leadership legacy she truly wanted. That simple step resulted in enduring feelings of personal fulfillment and well-being.

THE COACH IN YOU

"Character development," says educator John Agresto, as quoted in Thomas Lickona's *Character Matters*, "is not a spectator sport." Every day each of us is confronted with a near endless array of things in which we can invest our energy. The critical question is which of those possible investments will provide the richest return in personal fulfillment and meaning.

Once you create your character scorecard—though it's always a work in progress—you'll have your answer. Every day, in the different exercises you'll do, you'll be building the strength of your moral character. You'll make mistakes. You'll refine. You'll build "muscle." *All the time.* In doing so you'll avoid the anthem—to paraphrase the famous line from *Glengarry Glen Ross*—that destroys men's lives: "ABC, A—Always, B—Be, C—Closing, Always Be Closing!" For you, it'll be: "ABC, A—Always, B—Building, C—Character. Always Building Character!"

Sound exhausting? In fact, you'll find it bracing and liberating. For one, you're no longer wasting your energy and time pursuing things that don't mean enough to you, breathlessly chasing triumph after hollow triumph. "The moment of victory is much too short to live for that and nothing else," said champion Martina Navratilova, who should know, since she experienced more victory than any female tennis player ever. With this new scorecard, you are no longer spending energy on determining why it is you're doing what you're doing, because you have defined an ultimate purpose that holds up to scrutiny. In fact, you will find it magnificently energizing when what you do—when *everything* you do—serves the purpose of helping you to get ever closer to the ideal you have set for yourself.

When we really want something, we invest our energy in greater quantity and with greater quality, focus, and intensity. It is within our control to stop investing energy in things that are not fulfilling and begin investing in things that are. If, for example, you want to overcome narcissistic tendencies, you must build your capacity for compassion, humility, and gratitude by investing your energy directly in them. This is not to say that it's easy or that it happens quickly. It isn't and doesn't. But that is how change occurs: in response to an intentional change in the course of energy.

As you purposely invest energy in this new character-centered way, you are training your "inner coach." Through the scorecard tools, tests, and inventories provided throughout this book, your "inner coach" will become more skilled in ensuring that you act, first and foremost, with ethical consideration. Your inner, private voice—the one that too often in the past wondered "What should I do here?" or "What am I doing?" or "Is this who I want to be?"—will start to sound different. It will counsel you, through the lens of both your Ultimate Mission and your character scorecard, on what to do and what not to, on the big things and the small. It will coach you on the difference between that which you want to have versus that which you need to have. Over time, when trained properly, this voice in your head will deliver sound, wise, compassionate, tough, and confident self-coaching.

"Compared to what we ought to be, we are only half awake," wrote William James. Change the scorecard and you change the flow of energy. Change the flow of energy and you change the whole game.

TRAINING CHARACTER MUSCLES

Building character is analogous, as I've said, to building muscle. Fundamentally, muscles grow in response to energy investment. To increase the functional strength of the bicep muscle, for example, one must find ways, such as weight lifting and other forms of exercise, to stress the bicep beyond normal limits. When repeated, this increased energy investment stimulates new growth because it sends a message to the system that more bicep muscle is needed for the person to function optimally in his or her environment. The name we give such intentional increases in energy investment? Training.

Conversely, when you cease making energy deposits in a muscle, atrophy begins almost immediately—precisely what happens when an arm or leg is placed in a cast. As soon as the cast is applied, the muscles protected by the cast begin losing their functional capacity to exert and resist force. After the cast is removed, you regain functional strength in the atrophied muscles by exposing them to gradual, progressive doses of stress, or energy investment. The name we give for this? Physical therapy.

Just as the muscles of the body must be regularly exercised to maintain or grow physical strength, so must the muscles of integrity, honesty, gratitude, humility, respect for others, etc., be exercised to maintain or grow character strength. Use it or lose it. It's that simple.

In his book *The Talent Code*, Daniel Coyle writes about how we gain proficiency at all kinds of skills through a similar mechanism: "The more we generate impulses, encountering and overcoming difficulties, the more scaffolding we build. The more scaffolding we build, the faster we learn." This is true in the quest not only to become a better violinist or a better swimmer, but also a better person. Coyle refers to "deep practice," which "takes events that we normally strive to avoid—namely, mistakes—and turns them into skills." Physical competency (and eventually brilliance) is built on repetition, adaptation, and experience, including the mistakes and the lessons we learn from them. Why wouldn't character competency (and eventually brilliance) be built on that, too? In his book *Flourish*, Martin Seligman talks (as he and Christopher Peterson have done previously) about implementing "signature strengths"—identifying character traits that one is already pretty adept at, and finding ways to deploy and enhance them further.

Not only will you feel intrinsic value as you build new strengths, you can be chemically rewarded for the effort as well. Just as working out at the gym produces a cascade of pleasing hormonal releases, including dopamine, so, too, dopamine can be "trained" to release in response to acts of character.

As with workouts for the body, the more you train, the stronger you become; the stronger you become, the better equipped you are to make the right choices; the better equipped you become to make the right choices, the more you avoid looking outward at society's metrics of success, including parents' expectations and employer's demands, for your own satisfaction.

TRAINING DEPOSITS THAT BUILD CHARACTER STRENGTHS

What follows are eight important ways energy can be invested to spur character growth. (Note that some of these work for adults or children, while some are more geared for parents to use with children.)

1. Modeling

When you model patience, humility, dependability, self-control, etc., you stimulate growth in these character dimensions not only in yourself but also in those who witness it. Stimulating the visual sense causes energy to flow in the direction of the modeled virtue being observed. The brain possesses hundreds of billions of synaptic connections, all of which represent pathways for electrochemical energy impulses to travel. Each time an energy impulse is sent down a particular pathway, the pathway (circuit) is strengthened and the functions associated with that pathway are activated.

For me, I will never forget, as a kid, watching my father work for hours and hours on our family's taxes, and the meticulous way he documented everything. He had always talked to me about integrity and honesty, about the unacceptability of lying, about how you did what you said you were going to do. But nothing made a deeper impression on me than actually watching him do this. Each year, he was determined not to underpay or overpay his taxes by a penny. He would bend no rule. He never looked for loopholes or questionable deductions. If he had any doubt, he would give the government the benefit of it. "I want to be fair," he'd tell me, so I understood what he was doing and why. The experience taught me unforgettable lessons in ethical behavior—about fairness, humility, gratitude; about doing what was right, not what was expedient. In my case, seeing was believing. It made my father's words come to life, and they now live on in me.

2. Talking

Repeatedly talking about the importance of a particular character trait, such as honesty, compassion, having a positive attitude, causes energy to flow in the targeted character direction. The more parents, teachers, coaches, and managers reference character traits in their everyday conversations, the more they give life to the strengths discussed, and to their primacy.

For example, when people who are in a position to influence others witness an act of kindness, politeness, generosity, or selflessness, be it with family members, colleagues, or complete strangers, they should acknowledge the noble act by talking about it publicly with those they wish to influence. Even when lapses in character are observed, the door opens for a short but powerful verbal reference or exchange that can stimulate the learning process in others.

3. Writing

One of the most powerful forms of energy investment for spawning new cognitive growth is writing. For twenty years, we've seen at the Institute how writing out one's thoughts and feelings by hand consistently contributes to lasting change. Researchers such as James Pennebaker, Karin James, and Virginia Berninger are helping in our understanding of how and why handwriting is such an effective instrument for cognitive and emotional learning. If asked what one thing they could do to best ensure that they will remember something, most people will choose writing it down on paper. By writing about the importance of a particular virtue and then giving concrete examples of how the virtue could be practiced in your life, you stimulate the neurological pathways that serve those capacities (increasing blood flow, oxygen transport, etc.). Andre Agassi discusses in his memoir how, after he found his way, he maintained his "steely resolve" by writing out his goals every morning. According to Agassi, "After putting them on paper, saying them aloud, I also say aloud: No shortcuts." By saying something terse and unambiguous, and writing it down, he proves the seriousness of his intent.

These exercises work even more profoundly in combination. Take writing and modeling, for example: After Cameron, one of our workshop participants and a sales VP for a produce company, returned to his home in northern California, he not only started to write down his desired behavior change but shared with his family his commitment to change. One day, he found out that his nine-year-old son had been in a fight at school and was going to be delayed the chance (rightfully, in Cameron's mind) to get his orange belt at karate because of it. (The boy would be allowed to get the belt he'd earned at a later session but not at the "graduation" ceremony with the other kids.) The boy was inconsolable. Cameron had the boy sit down and write up a "gratitude" list. After some crankiness and resistance, the boy came up with this:

I'm grateful for:
1. Arguments stopping
2. Sophia much nicer [the boy's little sister]
3. Going to Brazil (oba!!!) [the family had a trip planned]
4. You helping me better [the "you" is Cameron, his dad]
5. That we got new cereal yesterday
6. That I'm getting my new belt soon
7. Mom's good mood
8. My tongue brush [his mother bought him this the previous day]

According to Cameron, his son's demeanor changed almost immediately after he wrote the positive, self-affirming list. He perked up and apologized to the boy with whom he'd fought. He even asked his father to get him a notebook dedicated for writing up future lists, when the need arose.

As with any kind of important writing, scorecard diligence benefits from being repeatedly reviewed and revised. I look at my own scorecard frequently, and update it every few months. It's laminated, so that it can't be changed easily and is treated as something of value; it's right in front in my wallet, so when I open my wallet, the list is right there.

4. Reading

From Scripture to the great books, from a single powerful quotation to targeted affirmations, reading is an effective method of learning about and ultimately cultivating character. Books that employ action heroes that display strong ethical character traits can be particularly effective. There is no shortage of material: Greek myths; Aesop's fables; Christian parables; *Pirkei Avot* (*The Ethics of the Fathers*); many (though not all) fairy tales; many action-hero children's books; *1984* or really anything by Orwell; almost anything by Hans Christian Andersen, C. S. Lewis, or E. B. White; *To Kill a Mockingbird*; biographies of Lincoln, Harriet Tubman, Jackie Robinson, Eleanor Roosevelt, and Joseph Campbell to mention just a few.

5. Storytelling

Closely associated with reading as a tool for strengthening character is storytelling. We're storytellers by nature and necessity. One of the important ways we learn is by listening to the stories others tell; and we learn by formulating our own stories, about how and why things happen. Can there be a better way to move us to be more values-driven in our behavior, to be more loyal, just, courageous, honorable, etc., than for us to hear an emotionally charged story in which such values are central and celebrated? (Indeed, propaganda exists and thrives for precisely this reason—because emotional stories about the values the propagandist wishes to glorify, be they positive or negative, can make us move mountains.)

From epic movies to book classics, storytelling can be a powerful tool for teaching character strengths (*A Few Good Men, Saving Private*

Ryan, Dead Poets Society, Braveheart, King Arthur and the Knights of the Round Table).

6. Debating Moral Dilemmas

The psychologist Lawrence Kohlberg strongly advocated teaching character through the presentation of moral dilemmas. *Here's a set of circumstances—now tell me: What's the ethically right thing to do? What criteria should we use to help us form judgments about right and wrong?* For example, you accidently learned of a serious safety violation in one of your manufacturing plants, a violation which was intentionally never reported. If you bring this to the attention of the managing supervisor, the employee will no doubt be fired. What is your ethical responsibility here?

In the course of a life, we must constantly make difficult moral judgments. It can be very helpful and instructive to write on paper the moral dilemma one might be facing and then list all the possible ways of responding. Prioritize each of the possible moral choices using your deepest values and best self as the template for deciding. Take your top choice and act on it.

7. Role-Playing

Role-playing is a surprisingly effective learning tool for all ages. From corporate skits to play therapy, having characters act out compassion, kindness, courage, persistence, justice, etc., causes energy to flow in the targeted direction and by doing so spurs growth. There is an intimate link between emotions and the physical body. Acting out certain emotions can cause facial muscles to move in specific ways resulting in actual changes in emotion. Researchers Paul Ekman and Harriet Oster demonstrated that facial muscles contracting in surprise, disgust, sadness, anger, fear, and happiness stimulated emotion-specific physiological activity. Looking angry, happy, etc., actually triggered changes in the physical body that corresponded to those acted-out emotions. Corporate skits that highlight moral dilemmas faced by employees can be very instructive.

8. Doing

The single most direct way to invest energy in a specific character muscle? Just do it. As Daniel Coyle writes in *The Talent Code*, "Nothing you can do . . . is more effective in building skill than executing the action, firing the impulse down the nerve fiber, fixing errors, honing the circuit." To grow compassion, for example, perform a random act of kindness every day for fourteen days, or volunteer an hour a week at a local hospital to work with disabled children. To stimulate the muscles of optimism and gratitude, have each person at the table say, before eating dinner, one positive thing that happened during the day.

THE OPPORTUNITIES FOR BUILDING character strengths are practically limitless. Suppose your scorecard requires you to develop the following character strengths: working hard, focus, having a (more) positive attitude, and kindness. How many opportunities during the course of a day do you have to exercise each of these muscles? Whether you're a postal worker, a widget-maker, a CEO, a kindergarten teacher, or an airplane pilot, almost every hour of the day presents opportunities to sharpen one or more of these, including saying thank you, letting others go first, opening doors, writing thank-you cards.

One might argue that a nurse or kindergarten teacher has more daily opportunities to work on her or his compassion or patience than a CEO or plumber, but is that so? Your environment is what you make of it. Showing kindness in your somewhat less supportive environment (your Wall Street job or customer complaint call center) brings returns that are commensurate with the situation. Maybe you're in an environment that doesn't push you to exhibit patience or honesty or optimism, but when you actively do so, it pays even greater dividends for your character. A traffic jam and several jerky drivers cutting you off presents you, in fact, with a great petri dish for exercising self-control. Like they say about New York: If you can make it there, you'll make it anywhere. You don't grow patience while lying in a hammock on your favorite beach.

And that's one of the great secrets that should never have been a secret: When you have "everything"—money, power, prestige, fame, beauty, access, etc.—it can often be pretty darn hard to hone your moral character skills. Because you're not being tested in the same way, it may be much, much harder for you to do so than the person in a dead-end job, the person who has no chance for a financial windfall, the mother whose kids are screaming and fighting the moment she walks through the door, the father who's never around because he's always working, the unemployed worker who sees bills piling up on the table. I do not intend to suggest that such stresses are not part of the playing fields of highly successful C-level and other executives; only that their lives of significant means can ameliorate the stresses substantially.

As mentioned earlier, the key to happiness has little to do with external circumstances (10 percent or less). The key to happiness and fulfillment is intrinsic, and that is *always* within one's reach because it is always inside you. Practically every week I see executives who fail to embrace this critical understanding intellectually or emotionally.

You may never reach some of the goals you have for yourself— extrinsic *or* intrinsic—but creating a new scorecard and following it drives home the importance of fully immersing yourself in your life *however it exists*. The scorecard reminds you daily that there is no benefit to waiting for your happiness until tomorrow comes with more promise. As good as it gets can still get better.

INVESTING EFFORT VS. INVESTING ENERGY: WHAT'S THE DIFFERENCE?

The difference between the right word and the almost right word, wrote Mark Twain, is the difference between lightning and a lightning bug.

So, too, with the words "energy" and "effort": They sound as if they can be swapped for each other, yet for us at the Institute, the difference between them is significant. Investing one's best effort has a very different meaning from investing one's best energy. Best effort simply refers to the quantity or volume of energy invested. Energy, including human energy, possesses quantity, quality, focus, and intensity. It's pretty clear what quantity means, but how about quality? Just as gasoline has an octane rating (connoting quality) from low to high, human energy also possesses quality. The highest-quality energy comes from hormonal releases associated with positive emotions such as hope, optimism, challenge. The lowest-quality energy comes from hormonal releases associated with negative, survival-based emotions, such as anger, fear, guilt, jealousy, and revenge. You might invest your best effort in terms of quantity, but if your effort is tainted by hormonal releases associated with anger or fear, then the investment value will likely be reduced. Human beings function optimally in the presence of positive emotions.

The same is true of focus. Even if you make your best effort, if it is made in a scattered and unfocused way—while multitasking or thinking about the consequences during the event, for example—then you will receive a much lower return on that energy investment than if it were concentrated and focused.

The fourth dimension of energy, intensity, is a measure of the force of the investment. The stronger the force, the greater the potential impact. Intensity is also a reflection of commitment and purpose. Individuals can invest a large quantity of energy (best effort) but with very low intensity. Coaches often see this when their players are running up and down the field in a very carefree, purposeless way—when they're not playing with heart.

Carol Dweck and Martin Seligman have both talked about the primacy of effort in determining one's sense of well-being. I have found even their use of it limiting, because it refers largely to quantity, namely how hard one tries.

I strongly believe that it benefits us to expand this idea. Building

Four-Dimensional Energy

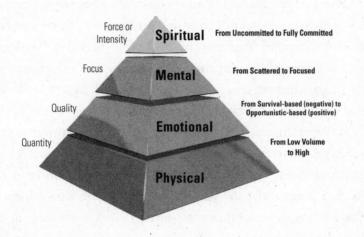

Force or Intensity — **Spiritual** — From Uncommitted to Fully Committed

Focus — **Mental** — From Scattered to Focused

Quality — **Emotional** — From Survival-based (negative) to Opportunistic-based (positive)

Quantity — **Physical** — From Low Volume to High

character muscles is best accomplished when one invests one's best energy in the character strength to be expanded. That requires the largest quantity, highest quality, most precise focus, and greatest intensity of energy investment possible.

WOODEN'S SCORECARD

John Wooden, the legendary UCLA men's basketball coach, oversaw an impressive amount of winning of the external kind: He won ten national championships, including seven in a row; led the Bruins to a record eighty-eight-game winning streak; and sent numerous players to the NBA, including several all-time greats. He was the first man, and one of only three ever, to be inducted into the Basketball Hall of Fame as both player and coach. The reason so many former players remember him with such love, affection, and respect, though, has to do with the immense intrinsic success he helped them—and himself—to achieve. He was legendary for never mentioning winning to his players, certainly not as the aim. As you get stronger as a person, he felt, you'll probably win your share, but the important thing is that your value cannot be taken from you.

His external success, the reason so many people have heard of the "Wizard of Westwood," was largely made possible because of the values-driven scorecard he created for his life both on and off the court. This scorecard, captured by his highly regarded "pyramid of success," was something he followed before he was well known, before he had a winning coaching record, and well before he won any national championships or became a legend.

What Wooden exemplifies is that energy investment must be multifaceted: physical, emotional, mental, and spiritual. When he spoke of poise, self-control, alertness, loyalty, or enthusiasm to his players, he modeled the strength in the reality of his own life:

Never strive to be better than someone else, because you have no control of that.

Strive to be better than yourself—every day.

Character is what you are. Reputation is what others think you are.

Never lie, never cheat, never steal. Don't whine, don't complain, don't make excuses.

These were all things he said to himself, as well.

More important than anything, perhaps, was the genuine care Wooden showed his players—as people first. His former players all say that he never used them to build his coaching legend.

How could he? His life scorecard would never allow it.

PART III

CHARACTER IN ACTION

6

It's Never Just a Job

Intrinsically oriented employees are more likely to seek out challenging tasks that allow them to develop new skills . . . thereby satisfying their need for competence. . . . While intrinsically oriented employees felt sufficiently energized after their day at work to participate fully in their family lives, extrinsically oriented employees felt mentally depleted after work, which impedes the development of a satisfying family life.

—MAARTEN VANSTEENKISTE, BART NEYRICNK, ET AL., 2007 BRITISH PSYCHOLOGICAL SOCIETY STUDY ON "WORK VALUE ORIENTATIONS"

He had achieved the absolute pinnacle of success, extrinsic success. It would be almost absurd, in fact, to argue that a human being could achieve or be rewarded much more than this man had: power, prestige, celebrity, access. The trappings of wealth. In those regards, he had everything.

"He owned a spacious ranch in the Texas hill country, a penthouse in Austin, a half-dozen cars fully equipped with telephones and traveling bars, a sailboat and speed boat, a movie theater on the grounds of his ranch and servants to answer his every whim," wrote someone who knew him extremely well. And the fabulously successful man certainly appreciated it. "You're dead wrong if you think that money and travel and nice things don't matter," he said.

Yet as his death neared, what were the man's predominant feelings?

Searing remorse. Disillusionment. Unhappiness.

His aide and eventual confidante, a woman to whom he had revealed his interior life as he had to no other, was privy to the vastness of the man's emptiness, which manifested itself in numerous ways—for example, how he concocted a different account about the life he had lived. "Visitors were sometimes surprised to find out later," wrote the confidante, "that narrative details, even entire stories, were untrue," despite the fact that "he usually had no practical purpose or motive for deception." Of the man's crushing loneliness, the confidante would later recall that he "could not bear to be by himself, not for an evening or for an hour. Always there were people, in his office, at his house, in the swimming pool, even"—how's this for loneliness?—"in the bathroom."

Upon retiring from his remarkably successful career, the man who (in the confidante's words) "had spent so many years in pursuit of work, power, and individual success . . . had no inner resources left to commit himself to anything once [that] was gone. . . . Retirement became for him a form of little death. . . . Once the realm of high power was taken from him, he was drained of all vitality. Years of concentration solely on work meant that in his retirement he could find no solace in recreation, sports, or hobbies. As his spirits sagged, his body deteriorated, until I believe he slowly brought about his own death."

About a month before he died, the man told the confidante that he feared that he was already being forgotten, that the contributions he had made to some very important initiatives, back when he was working, were being overlooked. "He was beginning to think that his quest for immortality had been in vain," wrote the confidante.

He spoke "with immense sadness in his voice," she wrote.

Then he said to her: "I'd have been better off looking for immortality through my wife and children and their children."

And the man died. Broken and unfulfilled.

The confidante?

Doris Kearns Goodwin, member of the White House staff and future Pulitzer Prize–winning historian.

The man?

Lyndon Baines Johnson, thirty-sixth president of the United States of America.

SAD AS LBJ'S STORY may be, it appears to be representative of one of our country's most pressure-filled leadership positions. Ronald Kessler conducted interviews with more than one hundred current and former Secret Service agents whose prime responsibility is or was protecting the president, vice president, and each of their families. Because the protection is twenty-four hours a day, seven days a week for the entire year, Secret Service agents have an unrivaled behind-the-scenes view of the character and private lives of those they protect. They know every visitor, every movement, every clandestine rendezvous. They often overhear private conversations, behind-the-back comments, and off-the-cuff trash talk after all the media and dignitaries have left the room. They see, as few people do, the unvarnished character dimensions of those they are protecting.

Kessler reported in his book, *In the President's Secret Service*, "You just shake your head when you think of all the things you've heard and seen. . . . They [the presidents] are probably worse than most average individuals. . . . Americans have such an idealized notion of the presidency and the virtues that go with it."

"The White House is a character crucible. . . . Many of those who run crave superficial celebrity," said Dr. Bertram S. Brown, psychiatrist and former head of the National Institute of Mental Health, aide to President John F. Kennedy, and a man who has worked with many Washington politicians. "They are hollow people who have no principles and simply want to be elected. Even if an individual is balanced, once someone becomes president, how does one solve the conundrum of staying real and somewhat humble when one is surrounded by the most powerful office in the land, and from becoming over-whelmed by an at times pathological environment that treats you every day as an emperor? Here is where the true strength of the character of the person, not his past accomplishments, will deter-mine whether his presidency ends in accomplishment or failure."

After conducting all of his interviews and reflections, Kessler con-cluded, "Unless a president comes to the office with good character, the crushing force of the office and the adulation the chief executive receives will inevitably lead to disaster. For those reasons, the elec-torate has a right to know about the true character of its leaders."

So it is with each of us. Life, in whatever form it takes, in what-ever direction it moves us, becomes our character crucible.

THE WORK MYSTERY

No one wants to end up like LBJ or any of the presidents these Secret Service agents describe. If anything, these men reveal the impor-tance of marrying work achievement and character. Both in and out of the office, work consumes so much of our time and energy that the way we manage ourselves during periods of high work stress, as well as in the day-to-day work world, goes a very long way to deter-mining what kind of legacy we leave and whether we receive genu-ine feelings of fulfillment from it.

The lesson to be learned here is not to devalue hard work, eschew the pursuit of achievement, or consider material possessions bad. The take-away is that, in and of themselves, such things leave us feeling empty. When, however, our work-related goals are beacons for a higher purpose—for making us better, more caring, more generous, more virtuous human beings and, by doing so, making the people around us, as well as the world, better—then they are actually neces-sary and vital in our pursuit of enduring value and well-being. By es-tablishing the primacy of character in our work lives, we can and will reap rewards above and beyond titles and money; such extrinsic dividends are not rejected or diminished but vitally *re-purposed* for something much more meaningful.

Take the story of Jessica, who began to realize how her sense of value came primarily from external achievements. She attended the Institute in May of 2010. She was forty-three years old, the mother of two boys, aged four and seven, and had been married for eleven years. She was a supply-chain manager for a mid-sized auto parts manufacturing company. By nearly all of society's qualifiers, Jessica should have considered herself a real success. From humble beginnings—a family of severely limited financial resources—she received a full academic scholarship to Vassar College, from which she graduated with honors. She went on to receive her MBA from Dartmouth, graduating again toward the top of her class. Her family of four lived in an upscale suburb of Pittsburgh, in what she described as "her dream home." The previous year her salary plus bonus had exceeded $300,000. Jessica's husband did some very limited landscaping consulting and accounted for no significant income; he was essentially a stay-at-home parent. Actually, it was a fortunate arrangement because Jessica's job required considerable overnight travel—approximately five times a month—to several of the company's Eastern and Midwestern locations.

Despite all her external success, Jessica reported little joy in her life.

Her greatest obstacle to being happy? Jessica saw her job as too demanding and too stressful. She perceived her greatest weaknesses to be her relentless quest for perfection and her critical attitude toward herself and others. No matter how well she did, it was never good enough. Her inner voice was a merciless critic, directed first at herself and then outwardly toward others. She frequently lashed out at members of her team for not working as hard as she did and not being as committed to excellence. The guilt she experienced over her frequent absences from home also took a heavy toll. And when she was home, she was too often frazzled—she could "drop at any moment"—exhausted from the demands of work, and emotionally distant, particularly with her husband.

The real dilemma, as Jessica came to see it, was that no matter how great her accomplishments, they never seemed to last. "No matter what I do, it's never enough to make me feel secure and worthy. I just keep chasing one accomplishment after another, hoping I'll finally feel good about myself." She was very disappointed in herself. She felt fragile.

Jessica was also tormented by the thought that if she didn't keep pushing the way she had been for years, she would lose her job (of this she was certain), which would result in financial ruin for her family. If she didn't continue to do what she was doing, everything would collapse. She was frightened by the specter of poverty for her kids: After all, as a child she had experienced it herself. For her children, she wanted better food, better clothes, better things than she'd had. If she couldn't give them that, then what kind of a mother was she? What kind of wife? What was the point of the hard work in college and chasing after her Dartmouth MBA? She was further terrified of financial ruin because she felt that her children would be unable to achieve her level of financial success. "The world is too difficult and different now," she said.

Jessica's case is not at all unusual. In fact, it's *very* usual. "The Ten-Page Résumé and I'm *Still* Not Good Enough" syndrome, as I call it, is commonplace. We'll hear more about her later.

CHARACTER AT HOME VS. CHARACTER AT WORK

Let's be honest: Working for both big companies and small can seriously test your character, even though you steadfastly want to do the right thing. Business is tough, decisions need to be made, numbers have to be reached. You may feel a distinction must be made ethically between what goes on at home and at work. The way you operate with family and friends, on one hand, might not be the way you manage and maneuver within a corporate setting. In the latter, you might well be expected to behave in ways you wouldn't necessarily choose on your own.

How many times have you made, or heard someone else make, one of the following statements?

- "That's the way they do business around here, always have."
- "As long as no one gets hurt, we do what we need to do to get the job done."
- "I don't have all that much say in *how* I do my job. I do as I'm told."
- "If we don't play by the 'rules' of the market, we won't have a company."
- "That's just the way everyone does business in that country."
- "The people who matter to me know who I am deep down, even if I do some things in the context of my work that no one would be proud of."
- "I make great money but I must play by their rules—it's a trade-off."
- "I'm not paid to be liked, I'm paid to get results."

In fact, such statements are made all the time. And those who make them are not necessarily morally reprehensible creatures. Hardly. I don't doubt for a second that those who say these things believe that if they really want to be successful, they have to play by the corporate rules.

Who can forget the scene in *The Godfather* where Michael Corleone plots the killing of one of his family's business rivals, along with a New York City policeman, and validates it to his brother thus: "It's not personal, Sonny. It's strictly business."

Going back to the very first pages of this book: When you imagine the twilight of your life and reflect back on it, what would a life of meaning look, sound, and feel like to you? Could it possibly include such equivocations and self-struck bargains like the ones listed above? Would it include admissions of compromises in your core values or breaches in your personal ethics? A small stretch of the truth to get a contract? A gift or payment to influence a sale? Insider information to make a buck? Spreading rumors? Overstating the proven benefits of a product? However disturbing it might be to answer these questions, they must be answered honestly if you're to solve the happiness/well-being mystery.

Again, I don't doubt that the vast majority of leaders and managers want to do the right thing. But it's hard. Many C-level executives come through our workshops and absorb our message about the importance of using everything in life, including one's job, to grow intrinsic character strengths. But once the idea sinks in, they will often say some version of this: "Great message! I get it and I'm on board with it—but it's not going to fly in the reality of the corporate world!" As one CEO put it, "How can there be such intrinsic value propositions in a completely extrinsically driven corporate world? You're saying that I should get my people to look first for intrinsic value when their very survival requires that we make our *extrinsic* fourth-quarter numbers? Are you actually saying I should get my people to position their jobs, first and foremost, to become better mothers and fathers and community leaders?"

My answer is *yes*. I say it because both my experience and the ever-widening array of research support it. The data show that when ethical values are given top priority, everyone wins: employees, their families, and, yes, employers.

A landmark 2007 study on "work value orientations," authored by Maarten Vansteenkiste, Bart Neyrinck, et al., and published by the British Psychological Society, found that "being predominantly extrinsically oriented not only entailed less positive experiences, but was also associated with more signs of unhappiness. Extrinsically oriented employees felt more exhausted and empty, and experienced the positive feelings that typically accompany the attainment of a particular work goal as less stable and more short-lived. Notably, all of these findings remained significant after controlling for various background variables." Furthermore, "having a strong focus on extrinsic, relative to intrinsic, life values is detrimental to well-being (e.g., lower self-esteem, vitality, self-actualization and social productivity) and is associated with greater ill-being (e.g., higher narcissism, depressive complaints) as well as poorer physical health." And: "Since extrinsically oriented employees tend to hang their self-worth on extrinsic outcomes . . . they are likely to feel pressured by ego-involved demands and stressful interpersonal comparisons . . . both of which thwart their need for autonomy.

"In contrast, because intrinsically oriented employees are concerned with developing their talents and potentials, they are more likely to take the initiative and actively participate in job decisions, thus facilitating their experience of autonomy in carrying out their job tasks." The authors concluded that extrinsically oriented individuals tend to over-idealize possession and wealth, and as a consequence, are more likely to persistently experience a sense of incompetence in attaining their values. Intrinsically oriented employees, on the other hand, are more likely to seek out challenging tasks which allow them to develop new competencies, thereby satisfying their need for mastery.

Equally important, research strongly indicates that "the negative effect of adopting an extrinsic . . . work value orientation was not limited to employees' jobs but . . . carried over into employees' life outside of work; extrinsically oriented employees reported lower life satisfaction, were less happy with their lives and experienced more conflict between their jobs and their family life. Perhaps, while intrinsically oriented employees felt sufficiently energized after their day at work to participate fully in their family lives, extrinsically oriented employees felt mentally depleted after work, which impedes the development of a satisfying family life."

The shorthand? Doing something for solely extrinsic purposes drains you of energy; doing it for intrinsic purposes energizes you.

The memo to executives might read: For your employees to produce their best, they need to be intrinsically driven and have a life beyond work. What Vansteenkiste and company found, not surprisingly, was that to perform optimally, workers—at all levels—must always be satisfying the three fundamental needs that Self-Determination Theory says they need: autonomy, mastery, and relatedness. There is no work, no matter the scale, that can simply replace that meaningful, intrinsically satisfying trio with another, extrinsically oriented one: money, title, and the corner office.

When our basic needs aren't met, work is reduced to a transaction; it's about chasing money and punching a clock, nothing more. On the other hand, when those three needs *are* met at work, the employee's talent and skill comes to life. In such a case, it hardly even matters what kind of job you have. Whether you are an airline pilot or a sanitation engineer, when you are able to exercise those muscles that want to be exercised, you will become more productive than you have ever been. It's one of the reasons branches of the military so consistently place in annual lists of happiest places to work. In a 2010 list derived from independent reviews of "blissful places to work" from CareerBliss, an online career-guidance tool, five of the top eleven slots were taken by the military—air force, army national guard, marines, navy, and army—which placed far ahead of companies like Microsoft and General Electric. Despite challenges that may occur when serving our country, including the possibility of being deployed far from family and friends, "the military provides many of the essential elements to finding happiness at work," says Bradley Brummel, psychology professor at the University of Tulsa, "including having a meaningful impact on the world, having true camaraderie with your co-workers, and having the opportunities to develop skills." Members of the military take pride in serving and protecting their country, for sure, but also get great satisfaction in the important work they do and the way they do it.

Is it really impossible to use work to grow new capacities that make employees better contributors both on the job and off it, as some argue? Organizations might greatly help their people and themselves—not merely their culture but their bottom line, too—if they engaged in "intrinsic value orientation training." In other words, companies could reap great benefit by encouraging employees to use their jobs to help them fulfill their deepest values and beliefs.

Charlie Kim, CEO of Next Jump, an Internet marketing company, sets aside specific time during workweeks for his employees to donate their effort and talents to a community project of their choosing. The premium liquor company Diageo engages in clean water initiatives in Africa and disease remediation in the Caribbean. Employees run for miles to raise money for charities and are sponsored by their company and fellow employees. These are but two of countless examples of companies helping their employees realize intrinsic success. Business leaders should seek out intrinsically oriented individuals whose core values are aligned with those of the company. As it stands, asking a potential new hire how a particular job could be a vehicle for expanding his or her character strengths and intrinsic growth opportunities is a very different conversation from the one typically carried on during the job interview process.

Some employees view their jobs fundamentally as a way to achieve financial success, exert control and influence over others, and attain status and importance. Others see their jobs as opportunities to acquire new competencies and skills, enhance personal interests, and make meaningful contributions to others and to society, while also achieving financial and professional success. Both hiring more intrinsically oriented employees and helping existing employees to move from extrinsic to intrinsic job orientations typically deepen overall engagement, resulting in enhanced business success.

Filling out the following form can help you assess the real value of pursuing a targeted extrinsic achievement. Every achievement requires that adjustments be made, that we adapt to the demands created by the pursuit. Some of those adaptations are aligned with who we want to be and some are not. The more aware one is of the adaptation forces, the more one can control the impact of the forces or even choose to discontinue the pursuit.

Take a moment and consider the impact your current job has been having on you as a person. Check the boxes below that most accurately apply. For instance, do you like yourself more or less as a consequence of your job? Are you more positive or negative as a result of your work demands and environment?

Assess the Impact of Your Current Job

Like yourself more ☐	☐ Like yourself less
More positive as a person ☐	☐ More negative as a person
More constructive inner voice ☐	☐ Less constructive inner voice
Greater self-confidence ☐	☐ Less self-confidence
Happier ☐	☐ Less happy
More focused ☐	☐ Less focused
More stable ☐	☐ More fragile
Less fearful ☐	☐ More fearful
Stronger character ☐	☐ Weaker character
More self-directed ☐	☐ Less self-directed
More humble ☐	☐ Bigger ego
More open to criticism ☐	☐ More defensive
More respectful to others ☐	☐ Less respectful to others
More disciplined ☐	☐ Less disciplined
More emotionally resilient ☐	☐ Less emotionally resilient
Love life more ☐	☐ Love life less
More grateful ☐	☐ Less grateful
Physically healthier ☐	☐ Physically less healthy
More ethical ☐	☐ Less ethical
More energetic ☐	☐ Less energetic
More excited about life ☐	☐ Less excited about life

Which column has more checks?

WINNING WITH CHARACTER

Nice guys finish last, the saying goes in sport (and is meant to apply to life in general). The corporate equivalent might be: Women and men of high character have more trouble reaching the top.

Our experience at HPI tells us that's not true at all. We look no further than the countless sport competitors we've had the good fortune to work with like Dan Jansen, Monica Seles, and Jim Courier, who display remarkable compassion, respect, and caring for others off the playing field and all became the best in the world in their sports. The notion that to be a great competitor, one must be a callused, cold, and ruthless personality is a most unfortunate misrepresentation of the truth. And the same holds true in the corporate world of business. You can possess great ethical strengths of character—kindness, patience, trustworthiness, care, and honesty—and be a fierce competitor. In fact, without these qualities, the doors to fraud and corruption open wide.

They can lead to tragic consequences for the organization. When leaders' compassion muscles are underdeveloped, they can take devastating actions like ordering layoffs, when less traumatic, but equally effective, cost-cutting measures—such as having all employees take a pay reduction—could have been implemented. When leaders' gratefulness muscles are weak, arrogance, a sense of entitlement, and hubris, all of which undermine employee engagement, can emerge. Just as every individual must possess and embrace an Ultimate Mission that clearly defines the moral principles that govern all of his or her behaviors, so must corporations have an Ultimate Mission, or code of ethics, against which all business practices and policies are vetted. Unless moral character strengths are sufficiently embedded in the DNA of a firm's leadership, unthinkable collapses are indeed possible—in some cases, perhaps inevitable.

THE ORGANIZATIONAL COST
OF MORAL MISALIGNMENT

As officers and employees of Enron Corp., its subsidiaries, and its affiliated companies, we are responsible for conducting the business affairs of the companies in accordance with all applicable laws and in a moral and honest manner.

—KENNETH LAY, CEO, ENRON

Having a mission statement is one thing. Living it is quite another.

Latin for "a set of fundamental beliefs or guiding principle," a *credo*—also known as a "code of ethics" or "code of conduct"—ostensibly provides an organization with a defined, sacrosanct set of ethics and rules of engagement. If a mission statement is to mean what it says, then it must have real impact on the behavior of the company's leaders. If it is to do that, then it must be aligned with the leaders' own Ultimate Mission and wider collection of beliefs. If it is to have meaning, there must be consequences for violating it.

The promise made above by Enron CEO Kenneth Lay was broken in spectacular fashion by the most successful and powerful employees of his company. At the time, Enron had grown to become America's seventh largest company, employing more than twenty-one thousand staff in more than forty countries. Its collapse in 2001 was the largest corporate bankruptcy in U.S. history until World-Com's the following year. In the process, Enron's shareholders lost $74 billion.

While Enron's code of ethics may have compelled Lay, for public relations reasons, to satisfy shareholders and to inspire employees—it certainly did not seem to compel him personally. And there's a precedent for this: In *The Smoking Gun of Enron's Code of Ethics*, author Bob Sutton writes of times when organizations spew out hypocrisy and dishonesty. Their frequent corrective? Have their leaders *say* the right thing, often and convincingly. In their minds, they are absolved of responsibility for the outcomes of their actions because they never intended to cause damage or destruction. This scenario is typical not only of companies in ethical distress but of individuals, too: While we tend to judge others by their actions, we judge ourselves by our *intentions*. Did Tyco's CEO Dennis Kozlowski and ex-CFO Mark Swartz, who were found guilty of stealing hundreds of millions of dollars from the firm, set out to be crooks? Did Adelphia Communications Corporation founder John Rigas and his son Timothy, who were convicted of bank fraud, securities fraud, and conspiracy after looting the cable company of millions, intentionally set out to be full-blown criminals? Probably not.

Many of the world's greatest atrocities have been committed under the guise of good intentions.

Again, according to Enron's Principles of Human Rights:

> As a partner in the communities in which we operate, Enron believes it has a responsibility to conduct itself according to certain basic tenets of human behavior that transcend industries, cultures, economics, and local, regional, and national boundaries . . . as we do not tolerate abusive or disrespectful treatment. Ruthlessness, callousness and arrogance don't belong here . . . when we say we will do something, we will do it.

Pretty inspiring, isn't it?

Some companies, on the other hand, just cut to the chase, forgoing all the inspiring language. WorldCom, which ultimately collapsed under the weight of its own moral decay, did not even bother with the ethical pretense. Their mission statement:

> Our objective is to be the most profitable, single-source provider of communications services to customers around the world.

The most important priority in WorldCom's statement is profitability.

Without careful qualifications, such a document can unleash powerfully dark forces so that the company operates *by whatever means necessary* to achieve the extrinsic goal. As Russ McGuire, online director of *Business Reform* magazine, points out, "Unfortunately, creating shareholder value is not really a useful company mission statement. It provides no meaningful direction to employees or managers. Unlike a mission that is focused on innovation or customer experience or serving God or serving humanity, a mission defined around wealth does not create a positive culture. Instead, it creates a culture of selfishness, greed, and results at all costs."

Even though WorldCom went off the rails, resulting in harm to so many people, can we blame them for being so up-front? Is profitability not the ultimate criterion of success for every public company? Does that not define what business success is all about?

Yes and no.

To exist and then to thrive, a company needs to be more than just profitable. Its success is linked to intrinsic values, whether the company wants it to be or not. Whether a company chooses to compete ethically or not has consequences—some intended, some not. One of these deeply personal consequences is how you feel about yourself, even if you don't articulate this to yourself every day as you leave the office to head home. To "compete" against some ethical standard is not to abdicate your company's competitive edge. It is not to say that your firm gets top marks for integrity while having its lunch eaten by competitors, who may not be quite as evolved. Demanding conduct consistent with high ethical standards does not preclude business excellence. On the contrary, sustained business success is possible only when competence coincides with fair play. Even Ponzi schemer extraordinaire Bernie Madoff could not sustain his unbelievable success absent at least the appearance of a moral compass.

Here are the mission statements of some real companies:

Create value for shareholders through the energy business.

—K ERR M C G EE C ORPORATION

Provide customers with the best value in energy and related services.

—WPS R ESOURCES

To be the most customer-centric company in the world, where people can find and discover anything they want to buy online.

—A MAZON

To manufacture and market high quality capital equipment designed to improve our customer's return on invested capital and/or in-use productivity. To be the most profitable machinery company in our industry as measured by ROIC for stakeholders. To be the most responsive company in our industry as measured by customer benchmarking and surveys. To be the best place to work in our industry as measured by employee surveys.

—TEREX

We are a market-focused, process-centered organization that develops and delivers innovative solutions to our customers, consistently outperforms our peers, produces predictable earnings for our shareholders, and provides a dynamic and challenging environment for our employees.

—ASHLAND

Profitable growth through superior customer service, innovation, quality and commitment.

—AGCO

Our mission is to enhance the company's core technologies through partnerships and strategic alliances with industrial consortia, universities, government laboratories, and unique research and development companies.

—AIR PRODUCTS & CHEMICALS, INC.

Are these powerful mission statements? Do they provide useful, ethical guidelines for how to act? More to the point, do these organizations have structures in place to enable and encourage ethical behavior from their leaders and workers?

I'm not suggesting that one or all of the mission statements above do or do not drive and inspire ethical practices. I am saying that each statement places a critical stake in the ground that will have ethical consequences for as long as these companies compete for market share, growth, and sustainable earnings. And having such a document is but one piece of the puzzle. Cultivating an atmosphere where employees actually believe in the importance of embodying a values-based mission statement is as critical as the mission statement itself.

HOW TO WRITE A
CORPORATE CODE OF ETHICS

When formulating a code of business, Joel Saltzman, a "corporate ethics trainer," recommends the following:

- Begin with an opening sentence that speaks to the company's general mission, values, and ideals.
- Make sure everyone knows the rules.
- Make sure everyone knows how to follow the rules.
- Establish a mechanism that ensures that employees are, in fact, following the rules.

Many large corporations have established values statements that powerfully guide the actions of leadership and those on down the chain. For his company's values statement, Sam Walton, founder of Wal-Mart, famously established three basic beliefs:

- respect for the individual
- service to our customers
- strive for excellence

Sam Walton believed that at the core of every rule or custom is the basic value of respect for customers, associates, and suppliers. Respect for others is Wal-Mart's prime focus for building relationships. Walton encouraged all associates to take this pledge with him: "I promise that whenever I come within ten feet of a customer, I will look him in the eye, greet him, and ask if I can help him."

. . . .

IN 2008, REPRESENTATIVES FROM Johnson & Johnson approached our leadership team. They were interested in possibly acquiring the Human Performance Institute.

I had always been impressed by Johnson & Johnson. As a global corporation, it had a soul; it had managed somehow, it seemed to me, to keep that soul as well as any similarly huge organization I knew of. Their code of ethics, called "Our Credo," was authored in 1943 by General Robert Wood Johnson, the son of one of their founders. The values expressed in their credo have guided the company's ethical decision-making through countless economic and political storms and now the recent "Great Recession." In the company's darkest public hour, the Tylenol crisis of 1982, when it was learned that someone had laced Tylenol capsules in the Chicago area with cyanide, their credo guided Johnson & Johnson and McNeil Consumer Healthcare leaders' decision to pull all Tylenol products from the shelves and stop all Tylenol production. Johnson & Johnson management believed so strongly in the precepts of their credo that they ignored advice from attorneys and consultants who argued that removing the product might harm the Tylenol brand.

The guidance provided by the credo, and the commitment to following it, enabled the company to behave in a way almost unprecedented in the annals of corporate catastrophes; a case study of the episode has become a Harvard Business School staple for exemplary crisis management. Chairman and CEO James Burke and Johnson & Johnson senior management based their decision to pull all Tylenol products off shelves on the responsibilities outlined in the first sentence of the Johnson & Johnson Credo:

We believe our first responsibility is to the doctors, nurses, and patients, to mothers and fathers and all others who use our products and services.

On a regular basis, Johnson & Johnson and its operating companies reinvigorate "Our Credo" for new and long-tenured employees by having them participate in "Credo Mapping" instructional sessions where ethical dilemmas are presented and employees must use "Our Credo" to help guide them to make value judgments. Employees are also routinely surveyed, anonymously, on whether they feel the company's leaders are in fact following the Credo in their day-to-day leadership activities and decisions.

IN THE ABSENCE OF an agreed-upon ethical code, lawlessness is sure to follow. But, while words have power, I don't believe values statements by themselves ensure ethical actions. Actions are guided by the deeply held, internalized beliefs and values embraced in one's story. For a corporate mission statement to get real traction in the lives of leaders, each leader must link his or her own grand purpose for living and the associated character strengths with the mission of the company.

When ethical considerations are removed from the corporate playing field, there is little hope for winning in a way that makes us all proud. Competition becomes unhealthy; our organizations become deformed. We become compromised characters. And it's easy to do, because temptation is strong. The prizes can be enticingly seductive. However, if you break your intrinsic value proposition—by keeping two sets of books, by failing to report the full truth to shareholders, etc.—whatever extrinsic value you achieve will be fleeting and unsatisfying. Break your intrinsic value proposition and you damage your organization and perhaps even your whole industry. Break your intrinsic value proposition and you damage yourself the most—physically, mentally, emotionally, spiritually. In business, as in all areas of life, when all is said and done, it won't solely be who won but how they won and at what price.

7

What Business Leaders
Can Learn from Sport

*It is not by muscle, speed, or physical dexterity that great things are
achieved, but by reflection, force of character, and judgment.*
—Cicero

For decades, I have worked with world-class athletes, and my
goal has always been to help them achieve as much success as
possible. The more success I had with athletes, the more opportunities I was given to work with people outside of sports, especially those in business. And the more I worked with non-sport
clients, the more I realized how the unique parameters of sport provided insights vital to people in most any high-performance arena,
from chess players to FBI agents, from sales managers to chief operating officers. Sport is a living lab for witnessing the role that character
plays in achievement, personal fulfillment, and life satisfaction. The
impact of big egos, hubris, selfishness, disrespect, distrust, dishonesty,
and disloyalty is especially visible. Precisely because the pressures are
heightened, the payoffs so visible, and the consequences for failure
so clear, the study of sport morality can be especially meaningful to
business leaders who want both to assess and build character strengths
in themselves and in their people.

It's also important to note that many of today's most visible corporate leaders credit their past sport experience for helping them absorb and navigate the pressures of corporate life. It's not uncommon, in fact, for companies to actively seek new hires who have been successful athletes. The big question is whether competitive sport does or does not serve to enhance the development of moral character in its participants.

I'd like to begin with a survey that has been given to nearly two hundred elite athletes once every other year for nearly a decade and a half. The survey, called "The Goldman Dilemma," presents the athletes with a hypothetical situation that challenges the core of their moral character.

The proposition goes something like this:

If you could take a magic pill that would (1) allow you to fulfill all your athletic dreams, (2) be a clear act of cheating because the pill is illegal, (3) be completely undetectable, thus ensuring you would never be caught, and (4) cause you to die within five years, would you take the pill? Yes or no?

Year after year, slightly more than half of the elite athletes say "Yes!"

How can this be? Competitive success such as winning an Olympic gold medal is so important to these competitors that they would not only embrace cheating in pill form but also give up all but the next five years of a likely long life? Dr. Bob Goldman, who conducted the multiyear survey, remembers warning one weight lifter of steroid-related health risks. The weight lifter's response? "At least I'll be huge in the coffin." How is it that such a significant portion of these athletes—who start out no worse as human beings than anyone else—have so completely lost their way that they would respond this way about some hypothetical magic pill?

Of course, the magic pill is not quite as abstract as all that. There are such substances, ones that elevate performance while compromising, even endangering, health, though in both ways not so neatly as the imaginary pill.

Evidence is rampant—at this point, depressingly commonplace—

that significant numbers of athletes are willing to compromise their character to achieve a sought-after outcome. What's going on here? Wasn't sport one of those pursuits we counted on to shape us to be the better people we meant to become?

I've witnessed world-class athletes who had successful professional careers and were quite fulfilled and others who had equally successful careers and were very unfulfilled. What did the former group understand that the latter group did not? After years of studying the research and amassing a substantial data set from my experience, I learned that the athletes who found fulfillment were those who used the demands of their sport to grow personal strengths that fulfilled important intrinsic needs. Unfulfilled athletes, by contrast, were those who used sport almost solely to pursue extrinsic rewards and, as a consequence, were unable to experience much happiness from the pursuit itself. For me, the critical insight was that fulfilled athletes used sport to build highly valued strengths of character, while the unfulfilled ones never made the connection. This insight, I have learned, applies equally to the world of business. Employees who found a way to use the stresses and demands of work to grow as persons, to become more aligned with who they most wanted to be in life, reported more life satisfaction and fulfillment. Repurposing work to grow inner strengths of character that flowed directly from their grand purpose in life was the key factor.

IT IS NO DOUBT disappointing, even shocking, for those who believe in the character-building benefits of athletic competition to learn that participation in sports can actually *undermine* moral character development. For example, a longitudinal study conducted at the U.S. Military Academy from 1989 to 1993 showed a decrease in ethical value choices over the four-year period for those involved in intercollegiate athletics. A 1995 study of 1,400 high school students found that nonathletes used a significantly more reasoned approach to moral dilemmas than did their athlete counterparts. Similarly, in

2004, a study of 595 students across all levels of college sport (Division I, II, III, NAIA) showed that nonathletes scored significantly better on tests of moral character than did athletes. And as the level of competition goes up, a 1998 survey showed, the level of moral reasoning and moral behavior goes down. In addition, males who participated at higher competitive levels for longer periods of time were more likely to legitimize rule-breaking and rule-violating behaviors. Regarding these lapses of character, a study of over 72,000 individuals from 1987 to 2004 yielded this "rather clear" conclusion: "The environment of athletics has not been supportive of teaching and modeling moral knowing, moral valuing, and moral action."

After reviewing all the relevant research, one can conclude that *ethical character building is not a natural consequence of sport participation.* Instead, sadly, *sports participation can actually erode moral development.* And, as I have learned, the same thing can be said about competitive business. When employees come face-to-face with the daily pressures to make their numbers, to increase market share, to out-sell, out-think, and out-perform their competitors, any preexisting character deficits in integrity, honesty, fairness, or the like make them very vulnerable to ethical lapses. Without great mentoring from bosses or supervisors that shore up existing flaws, such individuals will find that the relentless competitive pressure serves only to make their weaknesses worse.

PEARLS OF WISDOM FOR BIG-TIME COMPETITORS

In Chapter 5, I listed some of the formative ideas behind Society's Scorecard:

- *Winning is everything.*
- *Second best is for losers.*
- *Win at all costs.*

- *Show me a good loser and I'll show you a loser.*
- *When it's all said and done, winning is what matters.*

These bromides can be heard not only in the locker rooms of sport but in the corridors of business, as well. If these are the barely veiled messages of coaches and supervisors, then how can we be surprised when we discover self-absorption and cheating in many forms? How can we not expect competitors to feel as if their sense of self-worth is defined at least partly, if not largely, by their extrinsic results? One thing is certain: The more a person's identity becomes linked to winning and losing, the more likely he or she will bend or distort moral principles to survive psychologically. When the belief takes hold that winning changes everything, that in fact winning *is* everything, then ambition can turn ugly very fast (e.g., parental fist-fights in the stands, intentional injury to one's opponent [à la Tonya Harding, Mike Tyson], lying, cheating, and even criminal fraud).

Put yourself in the shoes of Mark, a young tennis player whose essential sense of value comes from his coach:

> *When I was winning, I seemed to be everything to my coach; I felt I could do anything. When I started not playing very well—I don't know why—and had several bad losses, and then some more, he just gave up on me—and started giving his attention to others who were winning. I started trying harder and harder to win so that he would come back to me and believe in me again, but I haven't been able to stop the losing. I just get too nervous when I compete now and I've lost all my confidence. I feel like my life is coming apart.*

What might a young athlete like Mark do if the opportunity to regain his winning presented itself? How much of his character would he be willing to compromise to regain his sense of value and self-worth, the attention and "love" of his coach? In an article in the *Journal of Psychology of Sport and Exercise* titled "When Winning Is Everything: On Passion, Identity and Aggression in Sport," the authors found that when young athletes have an obsessive passion for a sport, they are more likely to show aggressive behavior, especially under identity threat, when their self-worth is under siege. They concluded that "the love for one's sport may lead to some maladaptive interpersonal behavior, especially if such love is rooted in a sense of identity that is contingent on doing well in that sport."

Given all this, how hard is it to understand that an elite athlete might opt for a magic pill? And how hard is it to understand that employees who base their perceived value fundamentally on work factors not under their direct control, such as making sales quotas or becoming top producer, will not only struggle with persistent feelings of insecurity and self-doubt, but also may display, from time to time, antisocial and aggressive behavior toward fellow team members.

"BRACKETED MORALITY" AND THE JEKYLL/HYDE ATHLETE

At HPI, we teach about consistency of actions and behavior. You can't act one way off the athletic field and another way on, in the same way that in business you can't be ethical at home and somewhat less so at work. Character is not a cloak you can take off and put on at will.

In football, is it okay to cut the legs out from someone? How about trying to make him tear his ACL? Is that wrong? Or is it smart football? Or both? In business, is it okay to spread highly destructive rumors about a competitor to get that competitor to implode?

As they embarked on their landmark study of athletes, "Moral Reasoning in the Context of Sport," David Shields and Brenda Bredemeier, codirectors of the Center for Sport, Character and Culture at the University of Notre Dame, came up with the following, rather groundbreaking conclusions about the moral reasoning of athletes while engaged in competition. As you read them, consider how many of them might also apply to the workplace (my italicized version).

- Competitive sport can produce radical changes in the way athletes perceive right and wrong.
- *Competitive business can produce radical changes in the way employees/ leaders perceive what's ethical and what's not.*
- "Game reasoning" allows athletes to separate sport morality from everyday life morality.
- *"Game reasoning" allows employees/leaders to separate business morality from everyday life morality.*
- The context of sport allows athletes to be "released from the obligations to think of others."
- *The context of competitive business allows employees/leaders to be released from the obligations to be kind or compassionate toward others.*
- When winning is granted top priority, the goal to emerge victorious outweighs any moral or ethical considerations.
- *When closing the deal, making the sale, etc., is granted top priority, the goal to emerge victorious can outweigh any moral or ethical consideration.*
- Sport competition opens the door to "bracketed morality, where a completely different standard for moral reasoning applies. This is captured best in the statement "Give sport participants a moral inch and they'll take a mile."
- *Competitive business opens the door to "bracketed morality" where a completely different standard for moral reasoning applies. This is captured best in the statement "Give employees/leaders a moral inch and they'll take a mile."*
- Because of the phenomenon of "bracketed morality," sport does not build moral character. Sport participation can be used to enhance moral development, but the purpose and meaning of sport competition must be completely redefined and restructured.
- *Because of the phenomenon of "bracketed morality," the workplace does not automatically build moral character. One's job can be used to enhance moral development, but the purpose and meaning of achievement must be intentionally redefined and restructured.*

Once, we might have thought of the field, the court, the course, the rink as an ideal place to, if you will, "practice real-life morality," without the bother of life-and-death consequences. It turns out, though, that people's behavior may actually turn uglier in those arenas, not more noble. Perhaps it's the abstraction of athletic competition that enables participants to do this.

Not all sports, I have learned, are created equal: Golf continues to demand of its participants, for various reasons, a higher level of accountability and civility. Also, studies have shown that competitors in team sports—for reasons that are somewhat mysterious, even counterintuitive—tend to behave worse in the heat of battle than those engaged in individual sports. Perhaps because the spotlight is not just focused on a single competitor, a player is more likely to cross an ethical line because he or she may not get caught. In individual sports, cheating is too easy to catch.

Is it really that surprising that the notion of "bracketed morality"—or "situational ethics," as it is sometimes referred to—applies to business as well as sport? Human beings have a remarkable ability to compartmentalize their ethical standards in ways that can have tragic consequences. Soldiers in Nazi Germany would, after perpetrating unthinkable acts of concentration camp cruelty, return home and be loving, kind, and empathetic with their family members. That same capacity enabled Bernie Madoff to defraud thousands of people and still be a loving, devoted father and husband at home. Have you ever witnessed a business colleague cross ethical lines at work and do or say things that would be unthinkable in the presence of his or her children or spouse?

"WHO SAID I'M HERE TO BUILD CHARACTER?"

The above words are an exact quote from a coach who took part in a two-day seminar held at the Institute in late 2010. Attending were many Division I collegiate coaches from throughout the country. I completely understood what the coach was saying, as well as these comments from his peers:

- "The pressure to win from fans, alumni, sponsors, press, and administrators is bone-crushing. If I don't win, the consequences for the school, my players, my coaches, and my career are catastrophic."
- "I went into coaching because I wanted to use sport to build character. That's all fine and good so long as I win. Who would care what John Wooden had to say about character if, rather than winning ten NCAA titles, he had losing seasons and no titles?"
- "Parents teach values, churches teach values, I'm paid to coach and win. Don't expect me to cover that ground as well."
- "Who I want to be as a coach and who I have to be to keep my job are worlds apart."
- "Coaches are paid to coach, not to teach values, for God's sake."
- "My greatest stress is having to coach players I don't respect, whose characters are seriously broken or flawed. I can't boot them from the team because I can't win without them. I end up helping them become superstars. I hate myself for leading people I don't respect to victory."

Would you ever hear similar comments in the world of business?

- "The pressure to make the numbers from board members, shareholders, and Wall Street is bone-crushing. If I don't meet expectations, the consequences for the company, my employees, my leadership team and my career are catastrophic."
- "A big reason for my wanting to be a business leader was because I wanted to use my influence to build better, more character-driven people. But if I don't make my numbers, I'll lose any chance I have to do that because I'll be removed immediately."
- "Parents teach values, churches teach values. I'm paid to lead and be profitable. Don't expect me to play morality cop as well."

- "Who I want to be as a leader and who I have to be to keep my job are worlds apart."
- "Leaders are paid to get results. Period. If you want kindness, compassion, empathy, or fairness, look elsewhere."
- "My greatest stress as a leader is having to lead employees and work side by side with colleagues I don't respect, whose characters are seriously flawed or broken. I'm actually helping them move up the corporate ladder because they make their numbers."

Fans pay big bucks to see their teams win. Pro sport is big business, and the business is unmistakably the business of winning. But how about amateur sport, particularly at the elite levels such as Division I collegiate competition? Clearly that's big business as well. Well-intentioned coaches often find themselves facing contradictory forces if they're going to keep their jobs. Stop winning and you're gone! Well-regarded football coach Jim Tressel's ugly departure from Ohio State University in the spring of 2011 was in part due to his failure to acknowledge to school officials that some of his players, including Terrelle Pryor, may have violated NCAA rules. Other such examples of moral compromise abound. The driving message, as one coach was told: "Have whatever philosophy you want, push character, values, goodness, or whatever. Just make sure the team has a winning season and contends for titles."

Coaches learn very quickly that they can get athletes to do almost anything by linking it to matters of character. After all, when you attack someone's character, you attack that person's central core of values. By associating issues of character with all the things they want their athletes to do, coaches can exert extraordinary control over their eager-to-please charges. Coaches link playing hurt, playing with pain, and taking big health risks with matters of character. When athletes play with pain, remain silent when hurt, disregard the warnings of the physiotherapist not to suit up, it shows "they obviously have great character." They're warriors. When athletes return to competitive play before they're supposed to, when they put their health and safety at risk for the team and the cause, not only do they inspire teammates to do the same, but they reveal their extraordinary strength of character. What young athlete can resist such a compelling invitation? The question I have for you is whether this misguided practice ever occurs in your company. Do employees forgo vacations, work when sick, give up planned weekends with family, skip breaks, work seventy-hour weeks to prove their strong character to bosses or superiors?

Equally misguided is the use of the collapse of character as the blanket cause for failure. When you win, you've got great character, and when you lose, you don't have enough. Authority figures quickly realize that attacking team or individual character cuts to the bone and rallies more focused attention. Business managers can use such character leverage to get employees to dramatically increase their commitment and effort. Challenging employees to "show me some character here and get the deal done" or "if you've got any character, you'll close the sale by the end of the month" will often get them to push harder and intensify their effort. The downside for invoking character in this way is that it does two things. First, it distorts the true meaning of character for the employee. He or she is not a stronger person of character if the deal gets done and not a weaker one if it doesn't. Second, it makes one's character contingent on outcomes that are beyond one's direct control, contributing to feelings of insecurity and inadequacy.

This power—to subtly or not-so-subtly link character with outward success or failure—is clearly unethical. Coach John Wooden, once said this about the power coaches can wield in the lives of athletes:

> *We coaches have great influence on the lives of all youngsters that come under our supervision and the life that we lead will play an important part in the life that they will lead. It is up to us that we regard this as a sacred trust and set the example that we know is right. We must try to prevent the pressures for winning scores from causing us to sway from the moral principles.*

According to Wooden's own players, he never mentioned the word "winning" in practices or before, during, or after games. He clearly understood the power of words in athletes' lives. Connecting winning with good character would have been unthinkable for him.

For today's coach to embody that ideal may require an almost superhuman effort. After all, the coach would be fighting society's ridiculously high regard for winning, fighting his or her own institution or organization's win-or-you-may-be-gone ultimatum.

Coaches with whom I have worked feel that pleas for more sportsmanship and character-building are outmoded. Times have changed, they say. Kids are different and the world is different today. I'm reminded of a comment by a college coach at a top university. "Where are the athletes who can take tough feedback?" he asked. "When I criticize them or say things that are on the rough side, it crushes them emotionally. Too many have no backbone. They're wusses."

Some coaches talk about the growing opposition to the notion that sport should ever be used as a builder of character. Some say that sport was never designed to be in the moral education realm. They argue that sport was intended to teach people how to win, to endure, to go through tough times, to be resilient. And what about business—was it ever intended to morally educate? In what way could its stresses be used to build character strengths in employees? What might be the impact on employee performance if character was given top billing on the scorecard of success?

DOES COMPETITIVE PRESSURE BUILD CHARACTER OR UNDERMINE IT?

When people learn that participation in sport or business may actually compromise moral development, it is often deeply disturbing. Why?

With all the leadership training executives typically receive, wouldn't it be logical to expect that the moral character of leaders would improve? Tragically, very little training is devoted to developing strengths of character like humility, respect for others, integrity, compassion, truthfulness, loyalty, or generosity. Leaders are clearly expected to possess such ethical strengths, but they are pretty much on their own to fill any deficiencies. When employees come to work armed with a full complement of moral strengths, they will generally navigate the competitive pressure with relative ease. They hold their ethical ground in spite of temptations to do otherwise. However, when employees come to work with ethical deficiencies, the competitive pressures may actually block or even undermine the ethical learning process—and stifle performance in the process. The best way to ensure that all employees possess sufficient ethical strength to deal effectively with the relentless competitive demands of business is to provide continuous character training for all employees. I'll discuss what that would look like in the next chapter.

PARENTS AND CHARACTER DEVELOPMENT

Parents play a pivotal role in how sport participation impacts the moral development of their children and provide a useful analogy for developing the character of employees.

As I see it, parents tend to fall into one of four buckets when it comes to character development and sports: protectors, challengers, pretenders, and firesticks. Protectors are those who believe the forces of competition are inherently damaging to self-esteem and character development. As a result, they feel compelled to step in from time to time to run interference and shield their children from the unhealthy stress, which prevents their children from using the forces of competition to build their character. Challengers are those who fully understand the powerful effect that competitive sport can have on children and are committed to using those forces as constructive vehicles for teaching both inner and outer strength. Challengers clearly get it: They understand that competitive sport for children is about development—physical, emotional, mental, and spiritual—rather than winning, and they are very active to ensure such development happens. Pretenders are parents who often sound like challengers in what they say, but send a completely different message through their actions: What really matters to them is winning. Firesticks make no bones about what competition represents: From Day One it's all about being on top, and they want their kids to be victorious, first and foremost. They push, scream from the sidelines, behave obnoxiously, and do whatever they must to get their children to succeed. Winning and losing is personal, for their kids and for them. Firesticks relentlessly push their children into sports because the ambiguity-free culture of wins and losses is ideal, they believe, for revealing to kids the ways of the real world.

My experience has been that these four buckets apply to business leaders as well. Protectors are those who believe the forces of competition and stress are inherently bad for the character of employees. They're constantly trying to find ways to protect their people from the stresses of rough-and-tumble business. Challengers are those who fully understand how the pressures of business can be used to forge priceless character strengths in the people they lead. Challengers understand the learning opportunity that's there. They see their most important responsibility as leaders as to challenge their people to never allow their ethical strengths of character to be compromised, regardless of the pressures to succeed. Despite what pretenders say, they care, first and foremost, about the numbers and getting results. Character development is fine so long as performance expectations are met. If employees have to bend the rules to get the job done, so be it. Just don't get caught. Firestick business leaders, just like their blood brothers in sport, make no bones about the fact that winning is most important. They push, threaten, and coerce team members to be victorious. Failure to meet expectations is simply unacceptable. Find a way, make a way, or harsh consequences will follow.

In their book *Whose Game Is It, Anyway?*, authors Ginsburg, Durant, and Baltzell argue that "organized sports give children the opportunity to face challenges that will help them learn important lessons about themselves and the world." Few would argue with the premise, but successful navigation through competitive sport requires full knowledge and understanding of both the rewards and hazards. Jack Nicklaus recounts a story when, as a young boy, he threw his club nearly as far as the bad shot he had just hit. His father walked up to young Jack, looked him straight in the eye, and calmly told him to pick up his clubs and go to the clubhouse—and that if he did what he did one more time, it would be the last time he ever played golf.

Jack Nicklaus's father understood how sport could be used to teach character lessons. The wisdom he imparted that created the most enduring value had far more to do with his son the developing person than with his son the developing golfer. Jack's father struck just the right note. He conveyed the message without breaking his son's spirit and helped his son learn to use the storms of athletic competition as character growth opportunities. Leaders can repurpose the storms they face in much the same way.

THE CHALLENGE PARENTS FACE IN TEACHING CHARACTER THROUGH SPORT

A little boy gifted beyond belief appears on the horizon. Not only does he fulfill his god-like athletic potential, but as he's racking up victories and championships, he exhibits a toughness, a resourcefulness, a focus that impresses us maybe even more than his technique and tactics. What's also noticeable, though far less heralded, is his poise. He's intelligent, aware of his place in the history of the game, and respectful of those who came before. He speaks lovingly of his parents, especially his father, and is obviously devoted to them. He espouses the values he credits them for instilling in him and has apparently kept himself from getting caught up in the bright lights of fame. Such things are quite impressive, but none of them will be the thing for which he will become incredibly famous and earn tens of millions of dollars. True, he exhibits a bit of a temper when competing—so maybe he's not a "good loser"—but then again, when did he ever have time to learn that? He barely ever loses. Nobody's perfect. This fellow hardly makes a misstep, both while he's playing and then after the contest is over. You'd be happy to have him for a son.

Only it then turns out, when he enters adulthood, he's not quite who we thought he was. We're shocked to hear about the number of times he's cheated on his wife, the gross indifference with which he's treated the sanctity of family, the blatant recklessness he's exhibited that's equal parts destructive and self-destructive. Turns out that for all of his amazing extrinsic accomplishments, there are some serious, indeed tragic, deficiencies in his mastering of a few highly specific character strengths.

Despite what I have just written, it is not my intention to bash the parental contributions of Earl and Kultida Woods, father and mother of Eldrick "Tiger" Woods. It is to spotlight just how difficult it is, in a society that values what it values, for parents first and foremost to cultivate in their children qualities that are rarely the ones valued first and foremost by society. There are so many forces at play. There is so much background noise. In some ways, the world is getting bigger, in other ways smaller, but certainly it's continually getting busier and more complex. Good parenting has always been incredibly difficult, but in some ways it's never been more perplexing and important than it is right now.

My experience has been that most parents readily admit that they show less excitement and enthusiasm when their son or daughter displays character strengths than when their children win titles, break records, or make the all-star team. Do you or your manager do the same? Do you recognize acts of extraordinary integrity, kindness, and graciousness with the same gusto and frequency that you show when employees make big, tangible things happen in the office?

JUST BECAUSE YOU SHOW UP EVERY DAY, HUSTLE, AND PERFORM IN THE CLUTCH DOES NOT NECESSARILY MEAN YOU'RE A GOOD PERSON

O. J. Simpson, Roger Clemens, Jose Canseco, Marion Jones, Floyd Landis, Michael Vick, Roscoe Tanner, Mark McGwire . . . the list goes on and on. The evidence is everywhere. One can become a star in sport, even number one in the world, and possess character flaws you could drive an eighteen-wheeler through, and the same is true in business. Unfortunately, for many people the extraordinary success *is* the enabler. All the fame, money, and accolades simply reinforce the idea that character deficiencies don't matter—not enough, anyway. Only when the character lapse results in something dire, like being fired or being indicted, does the individual find any motivation to address his or her personal flaws. As long as the success and money keep pouring in, as long as one is living the dream, why start identifying the holes in one's character, and doing the hard work of filling them in? What's the motivation?

Certainly there are athletes who possess extraordinary character, who are role models not merely as athletes and competitors, but as people—such as Dan Jansen, Monica Seles, Arthur Ashe, Payne Stewart, Grant Hill, Tim Tebow, Sam Bradford, Tom Gullikson, and Todd Martin. There are also countless examples of highly successful business leaders who possess extraordinary character and who serve as great role models for others—such as Peter Drucker, influential management consultant; Evelyn H. Lauder, former Estée Lauder executive; Steve Reinemund, dean of business at Wake Forest University and former PepsiCo CEO; Oprah Winfrey, talk-show host and media personality; Chip Bergh, CEO of Levi Strauss; Tom

Davin, CEO of 5.11 Tactical; Meg Whitman, former eBay CEO; Bob Carr, senior VP with GlaxoSmithKline; and Melinda Gates, cofounder of the Bill and Melinda Gates Foundation. But the extraordinariness of the people on both lists derives from the fact that the life of privilege they enjoy provides an unusually intense, nearly continuous battery of character tests. If the ethical character of these individuals had not been forged *before* the privileges and power began raining down, they would have had almost no shot at resisting the myriad character challenges that are sure to come.

CHANGE THE SCORECARD, CHANGE THE GAME

In golf, you have a scorecard. You know what par is for each hole. You know the distance to the pin. You know that the goal is to make the fewest shots possible. The scorecard determines how the game is played.

What if you used a different scorecard? Suppose, for example, the scorecard for golf changed. Instead of the goal being simply to amass as few total strokes as possible, now suppose the goal was a combination of fewest total strokes plus total time per round; the winner would be the fewest strokes in the shortest time. (The game actually exists. Maybe you've played speed golf before.) Adding the time element to the scorecard would dramatically change your competitive behavior, strategy, and physical, mental, and emotional training routines. The importance of aerobic fitness, stamina, running skills, footwear, diet, hydration considerations, and even the clothes you wore would be viewed differently. To win at speed golf, you would change a great deal about how you train and compete.

Suppose, as a business leader, your focus was not on the outcome alone—*Did you win the contract?*—but, most importantly, on how you did it. *Were you always truthful? Did you play fair? Were you respectful of others? Did you compete with honor? Were you positive and constructive with your team members? Were you humble in victory?*

Would the game not change dramatically for you? Would this new scorecard not enable you to receive truly lasting intrinsic fulfillment from your work as you used the forces of competition to grow in character?

This single insight changes everything.

8

Building Moral Character
in Others: For Business Leaders,
Parents, Teachers, and Coaches

Nothing can bring you peace but the triumph of principles.
—RALPH WALDO EMERSON

Up to this point, this book has necessarily focused on creating your own Ultimate Mission and a new, unique scorecard that focuses on a more fulfilling kind of achievement. The process of building character is a fiercely individual one, and only you know what success looks like for you. That said, I also believe that the process of building character doesn't end with each of us individually. From the employees we manage at work, to the teams we coach on the field and the kids we raise at home, many of us are responsible for the development and achievement of others. In these cases, we have a tremendous capacity to help these people jump-start their character development and improve their performance, often to the benefit of the company, team, or family, as a whole.

To take advantage of this important opportunity, this chapter will help you take the lessons found in this book and share them with those over whom you have influence. While you can't answer the questions for them, you certainly can, and should, help them understand why these things matter and how to start—not to mention share your own experience along the way. After all, if your performance and happiness increase because of this book, wouldn't you want the same thing to happen to the people you most want to see achieve?

HOW LEADERS CAN BUILD CHARACTER IN THEIR EMPLOYEES

Few leaders would deny that they want their employees to show good character, yet I frequently face resistance when I suggest that they must actively develop it. Given the fact that these busy managers and executives have to constantly update their teams on matters of strategy, goals, innovation, results, market share, and on and on, there's rarely any time, they say, left for strengthening their moral character. And even if they could find the time, they wouldn't know how to go about it—and why they should even try? As one middle manager said to me, "I don't really see myself giving a lecture on integrity, trustworthiness, kindness, or compassion to my people. I'd either get laughed out of the room or they would simply leave out of sheer boredom!"

"Just the idea of teaching full-grown adults anything about moral character seems somehow odd to me," said another very successful business leader. "It's like, why do I have to teach you this? You should have learned this long before now, and equally important, I don't have a clue how to do it."

Unfortunately, moral deficits do exist among employees, and those deficits can have devastating consequences for the businesses that employ them, as time has repeatedly shown. The fact that business leaders feel ill-prepared and uncomfortable with the area of employee character growth and development in no way minimizes its strategic importance to their businesses. Ethical deficits can and must be addressed by leaders in the same way they address all business imperatives, and this chapter will give you the tools to start.

ASSUME YOU ARE INTERESTED in helping your twenty-five direct reports, several of whom, like most employees, possess a few rather stubborn character deficiencies. You have no responsibility for how or why such deficiencies came to be, but now these individuals are in your hands. Some of these flaws are performance-based—e.g., being chronically late for appointments and meetings, poor focus, impatience, low self-esteem, and persistent negativity. Some are morally based—e.g., occasionally being disrespectful or arrogant, unkind or unfair, disloyal or lacking compassion. None of the deficiencies have reached a point where you feel removal from the team is warranted. From a talent perspective, this is probably one of the most successful groups you've had the privilege of leading in the last ten years. You would hate to lose any of them. What keeps you awake at night, however, is the impact the various character flaws might have on their future performance. You're particularly concerned about their moral deficiencies and how they might manifest themselves when work pressure mounts.

You have several questions regarding your involvement in the character development of your people. The first is how do you get people to confront their deficiencies without becoming defensive? Character issues are so personal, particularly those involving ethical behavior. Another question you have is, even if you were able to get your people to confront their deficiencies non-defensively, what could you do, practically, to help them convert their weaknesses into strengths? These are questions we have struggled with for years at HPI. The following step-by-step program represents our best answer to the important character questions posed by leaders. It is our belief that every company, small or large, should have a character development program, one that is central to their overall leadership initiative. Character training should be clearly defined, succinctly articulated, and skillfully implemented.

Here are the steps any leader can take to do that.

STEP 1: Provide all members of your team with a copy of the company's mission statement. The statement should speak not only to what the company aims to do (be profitable, return shareholder value, be the leading telecommunications provider, etc.) but how the company aims to do it (with integrity, with respect for others and the environment, with fairness, etc.). The "how" speaks to the values and the rules of engagement that govern execution of the company's business plan.

Discuss the mission statement and its meaning with your team. Do they find it inspiring? Do they think it serves an important purpose in the company's operations? Does it have historical value to the company? Discuss why companies have mission statements in the first place and what makes them work or not work from a practical perspective. Explore the extent to which the company's mission statement has been of value to the team members personally and what values are implicitly or explicitly reflected in the document. It's important that your team members believe that the values spelled out in the company's mission statement will help them be more ethical in fulfilling their job responsibilities.

STEP 2: Discuss the connection between your company's mission statement and the character of its employees, particularly their moral character. This is an excellent time to make the distinction between moral/ethical strengths of character and performance strengths. Make a complete list for each category and ask your people which should have the highest priority in terms of how their company and its employees operate. Ask them to describe scenarios where moral character lapses might occur and what impact those lapses might have on the company's future.

STEP 3: Have everyone craft a life mission statement. The goal is for every person to create the most succinct statement possible for how that person must conduct his or her life to be truly successful.

The concept of the Ultimate Mission, as we call it at HPI, was discussed in Chapter 3. Once every team member's mission statement is completed, each individual should identify the character strengths (both moral and performance) that are embedded in his or her statement.

While engaging in this exercise, you may note that defensive responses are fairly minimal. That's because you're asking your people what they most want in life.

STEP 4: Discuss any alignment that exists between the company's mission statement and the mission statement of each team member. Is there synergy? Are there conflicts? Are the character traits the company wants the team member to embrace the same as or similar to the ones the team member *wants* to embrace?

When there is alignment, it means that who your people need to be to succeed in life and who they need to be to succeed at work are one and the same, a true win/win. *Their job can actually help them achieve their life mission.*

STEP 5: Have your people write for ten minutes on their "best self." When are they proudest of themselves? What character strengths do they most embody? Next, have them compare their "best self" results with both their life mission and the mission statement of the company. Ask: To what extent are you at your best for the company when you embody your "best self"? This is another way to highlight the synergy that can and frequently does exist between employees' goals and those of the companies that hire them.

STEP 6: From their life mission statements and their "best self" exercise, have your team members build their own character scorecards. The scorecard should contain the top six character strengths each employee feels must be strengthened to ensure the success of the employee's life mission. The list should include at least three strengths from the moral/ethical category. Each person should ask the question, "In what areas of my character do I most need to grow to become the person I really want to be in life?"

Some companies are starting to link character assessment (both moral and performance) directly to employee performance reviews and compensation practices. For instance, the scorecard for employees of one company uses the following ratio for performance evaluation and compensation:

50% for what you accomplished (extrinsically based)

50% for how you accomplished it (intrinsically based)

STEP 7: Have everyone design a character-based weekly training log where every time an investment is made in growing one of his or her targeted character traits, it is recognized and recorded. As every successful businessperson knows, what gets measured gets done. Encourage your team members to make their scorecards highly accessible and to make entries on a daily basis. No energy investments, no new growth. Energy investments can be made by doing, writing, visualizing, reading, talking, and thinking.

Examples of investments that should be recorded in one's daily log:

- For patience with others: You intentionally fought the urge to interrupt a colleague who was taking forever to make her point.
- For kindness: You arranged to have dinner delivered for four days to a staff member who just had her second child and has few people around to help her.
- For humility: You intentionally gave the lion's share of credit to your team for completing a project, even though you ended up doing most of the work.
- For gratefulness: Once a week you thank a staff member for something he or she did.
- For integrity: You wrote in your journal for ten minutes on the meaning of integrity in your life.
- For compassion: You led a discussion on compassionate leadership with your team for ten minutes. Every week you start your team meeting with a short discussion on various ethical strengths of character. Your discussion topics for the next five weeks are (1) respect for others, (2) playing fair versus winning

ugly, (3) the cost of dishonesty, (4) generosity in the workplace, and (5) positivity as a competitive strength.

One of the most effective ways to strengthen the moral reasoning skills of your team members is to present them with hypothetical moral dilemmas that connect to the ethical challenges they will likely face in their work. Team members are to resolve the conflicts by using a combination of the company's mission statement and their own life mission statements.

STEP 8: Encourage team members to solicit real-world feedback regarding character deficits they might be working on—e.g., punctuality, respect for others, patience, positivity, gratefulness. Most character weaknesses are surprisingly visible to others, particularly those working closely with the employee. Soliciting "face the truth" feedback, as hard as it might be to digest, is critical to sustained growth.

STEP 9: Remind your people constantly that their moral character is especially evident when they interact with others. They communicate trustworthiness, humility, compassion, patience, kindness, and fairness through what they say and how they say it. Encourage your people to script in advance critical conversations they will have with clients and colleagues to ensure alignment with their deepest values and character commitments. Encourage everyone to share scripts with the team. When shared, make the scripts anonymous. Sharing scripts accelerates learning for everyone.

STEP 10: Model every character lesson you want your team members to learn. You must be living proof that one can re-purpose work to grow character. When you tell the truth and do so in a compassionate way, you model both truthfulness and compassion. When you avoid corporate spin and communicate from your heart, you lead with character. Your commitment to your personal mission and to that of the company should be evident in most everything you do and say.

STEP 11: Make ethical character the gold standard of your leadership. Acknowledge exemplary ethical behavior whenever and wherever you can. Two examples: "I loved the way you handled the conflict in today's sales meeting. You listened respectfully to Karen's thoughts and found a way to disagree with her without attacking her or putting her down—I was impressed!" And: "John, I was very pleased with the way you told the hard truth to the client today but did so in a respectful, understanding way. Terrific job!"

STEP 12: If someone refuses to grow, let that person go! If not addressed, deficiencies in character, particularly of the moral variety, jeopardize the entire business. Possessing moral strengths is not just a "nice to have" for employees, it's an imperative of the highest order. Make certain that the people you are leading get the message. Some messages you communicate can and will get lost. This one cannot!

HISTORICALLY, ATTEMPTS BY LEADERS to teach character development have been unsuccessful and unpopular. In no way should this fact discourage companies from looking for real answers. The stakes for everyone are simply too high. The final goal in the quest for character development is the creation of a corporate-wide culture of trust, integrity, respect, and compassion, one that can, at the same time, drive extraordinary financial success.

Every company should have a robust portfolio of best practices for employee character development. It is my hope that this book and our work at HPI will prove helpful toward that end.

HOW PARENTS, TEACHERS, AND COACHES CAN BUILD CHARACTER IN CHILDREN

What a profound thing it is for you to teach your child how to throw, to count, to read, to tie a shoelace, to drive. But nothing is more profound for a parent than to teach his or her child how to be a good person.

The three things parents most want for their kids:

- happiness and fulfillment in life
- strong moral character (the child becomes a good person)
- healthy, stable self-esteem

The true testament to good parenting is the building of great character and virtue in one's children, not whether they get into Harvard. Dan Jansen, the Olympic speed-skating champion, with whom I have worked, credits a lesson his father imparted that helped him to put competition and achievement in perspective. "I was twelve years old and pretty sure I was going to win the national championship," said Jansen, "but I finished second, and I cried all the way home on the drive from Minneapolis to Milwaukee. I kept thinking this great advice was going to come from my father to make me feel better. And when we got in the house, he said, 'There's more to life than skating in little circles.' And he left the room. It wasn't what I expected, but because it was my dad, I believed him. I always kept that in the back of my mind. Ten years later, when [my sister] Jane passed away and I fell at the Olympics, the words came back and I knew what he meant."

Most parents recognize that their kids won't make it into the professional ranks. Less than one in sixteen of all high school senior boys playing interscholastic football will go on to play football at an NCAA member institution. Approximately one in fifty NCAA senior football players will get drafted by a National Football League (NFL) team. The average career span is approximately 3.6 years, and "according to a 2006 report in the *St. Petersburg Times*, for every season a player spends on an NFL roster, his life expectancy decreases by almost three years." It's particularly hard for many parents even to recognize that this be-all, end-all pursuit of sports achievement might not be what they really want for their child, nor will they recognize it until the long-term effects begin to manifest themselves. (And maybe not even then.) They don't consider that, say, their daughter might have this to say about the relentless pursuit:

> *They have been pushing me from Day One to play tennis and be a star. I know all the money they have invested in my tennis has been hard for them, but it was their choice to do it. . . . When I win, I'm the greatest—they are so proud of me. When I lose, particularly to nobodies, they get angry, pushy, and walk away. I don't think they understand how hard it is to win. I don't lose because I want to. When I tell them that I'm not sure I want to play tennis anymore, they both go completely crazy.*

In sports like tennis, gymnastics, golf, and soccer, parents seize the opportunity to accelerate development by starting very, very early. By age five or six, kids show remarkable biomechanical skill and efficiency. As one highly educated parent said to me as we watched his six-year-old hit golf balls, "If Anders Ericsson is right, if becoming world-class at something requires ten thousand hours of deep practice, why not get the process started early?" By age fifteen, his son Kurt would be getting a development deal. "I wish I could have started my golf that early," said the dad, oblivious, I believe, to just how revealing his lament was.

Be it figure skating, piano, or hockey that their kids are immersed in, parents feel good about themselves because they are making extraordinary sacrifices and they have departed on the earliest developmental train possible. *Rather than goofing around in the early years*, goes the rationale, *why not get started now on those ten years of practice that will lead to something? Lily may not like all the hard work now, but when she gets really good, she'll thank us.*

As parents, we act instinctively, lovingly. But we may not be working off of a scorecard consciously designed to build virtue in our children. My three sons are now grown, but had I known when they were little how well it would have served me and them to have a character scorecard in place, I have no doubt that we all would have accelerated the learning curve.

Few parents have such a character scorecard they're working off of. The vast majority live hectic lives day to day, doing what they can while hoping things turns out well with their kids. It's rare for children's character education to be addressed explicitly—and so most parents cross their fingers and hope that character forms out of their kids' everyday interactions in school, playing sports, religious education, etc.

Or you can be more conscious and intentional about it. You can look for ways to accelerate, focus, and deepen your children's character education. You can take closer stock to see that character flaws aren't forming or ossifying. You can help make a scorecard for them.

When? Perhaps the more pressing question is: How many days do you have to form the character of your child?

It gets started faster than you think. Social conditioning begins from Day One—so it's important from the beginning to get character-teaching right. Of course, the lessons must be age- and stage-appropriate. The scorecard for a four-year-old will look very different from the one for a seven- or eleven-year-old. You can't expect ethical development until a certain level of intellectual development allows it to bloom. By creating a scorecard for your child, you can help guide him or her to choose a meaningful mission, to determine an ultimate purpose, to begin to shape his or her personhood. Early on is the best, easiest time to start. Suppose the child displays gratefulness but shows consistent lapses in honesty: A good way to strengthen that child's sense of honesty in the early years is to define your core values and keep track of them. By starting the practice early, you make character the focal point of everything that happens to your child (and to you). With their scorecard in hand, your kids will remember the importance, both generally and specifically, of strong character throughout their lives. And as they develop, they will naturally seek out opportunities for autonomy, mastery, and relatedness (purpose). Thus they'll start to take more and more ownership of that scorecard.

WHEN KIDS AND THE PRESSURE TO ACHIEVE COLLIDE

The pressure to achieve begins young and continues throughout adulthood. The statistics on high school student cheating are breathtaking: Of those included in *Who's Who Among American High School Students* (2000 edition), 80 percent admitted to cheating. In the "2002 Report Card on the Ethics of American Youth," from the nonprofit Josephson Institute for Ethics, a similar percentage—75 percent—admitted to "cheating on an exam in school during the past year." Yet what I find more telling, as Thomas Lickona keenly observes in *Character Matters*, is those statistics set against two other stats from the Josephson survey: 76 percent said they had high "ethical self-esteem" while almost 80 percent agreed that "it's not worth it to lie or cheat because it hurts your character." Weighed together, these answers seem not to align. The disconnect between thought and action appears vast.

When it comes to the age at which kids cheat, the habit reaches forward and backward. In a more recent survey from the Josephson Institute—from early 2011—one-third of U.S. high school students admitted to using the Internet to plagiarize. A 2009 study in *Ethics & Behavior* reported that over 80 percent of a sample of college alumni said that as undergraduates they had engaged in some form of cheating.

According to the 2010 CIRP Freshman Survey, UCLA's annual report on students entering four-year U.S. colleges and universities, the percentage of students who rated their drive to achieve highly has been trending upward (almost 76 percent assessed their drive to be "above average" or in the "highest 10 percent"), while their self-reported emotional health has been trending downward (barely more than half put themselves in those two categories).

Many of the same things we want for ourselves—many of the same extrinsic achievements—we want for our kids. The problem? The urge, while loving and well-meaning, is also potentially more toxic. Precisely because you want someone else to achieve these things, someone over whom you have great influence, your child is being pressured to accomplish goals that are *doubly* extrinsic: achievements that are (a) only temporarily satisfying and (b) being pursued largely to satisfy someone else—you, the parent. The possibility of experiencing the satisfaction that comes with intrinsic accomplishment seems all the more remote for such children.

To meet the need (our need) for our children to achieve, these are some of the messages we convey, explicitly or not:

- Make something of yourself by creating a tangible trail of verifiable accomplishments.
- Waste no time, make every second count: Somewhere in the world someone is gaining ground on you.
- It will all be worth it in the end. So what if you have no life now? Someday you will be happy and find peace when the goals are all achieved.

Parents who as kids did not take advantage of every waking moment to excel and "make something of themselves" often act particularly determined not to make that "mistake" with their children. Because they are deeply focused on the task at hand, they're unlikely to confront fully the *counter*argument to each of the three points above, namely:

- Is the "success" of your child to be measured primarily in verifiable accomplishments? Exclusively? When your children don't achieve, what does that mean about who they are? And who you think they are?

- When are kids allowed just to be kids, to play and have fun and enjoy their lives? Yes, there are many people always out there studying hard to get ahead, but must childhood and adolescence be sacrificed in order for your kids to take on the world?
- If the addiction of achievement never gets satisfied, then doesn't it follow that the rat race never ends? And continues until death?

If the parents who advocate the above sound familiar, maybe it's because they sound like "Tiger Moms" (and "Tiger Dads"), the sort of parent that Chinese-American law professor Amy Chua wrote about so controversially in her 2011 book, *Battle Hymn of the Tiger Mother.* In it, she spoke of the great value underpinning the Chinese Tiger Mom—style of parenting, which included rules for her children such as no playdates or sleepovers; no involvement in school plays; no complaining about not being in a school play; no watching TV or playing computer games; no choosing your own extracurricular activities; no getting any grade less than an A; no being anything but the number one student in every subject except gym and drama; and no playing any instrument other than piano or violin. The not-at-all-veiled message of this parenting style: *One day, you'll thank me (you might even thank me while it's going on), because no one out there will outperform you.*

The main reason the book and its advice achieved such notoriety, I think it's fair to say, is because of its inherent critique of a more "Western," particularly American, style of parenting, which was seen as one in which children are coddled to such an extent that they are unprepared to compete in the real world and overpraised into unreality. (Interestingly, the popular term "helicopter parent"★ may really be applied to both the Tiger Mom *and* this more Western type of parenting.)

As for the approach of the Tiger Mom, our experience at the Institute is that you pursue such an agenda at your and your child's

---

★ A parent who pays extremely close attention to his or her child's experiences and problems.

great peril. If achievement is the template against which you measure your child's success, as well as your success as a parent, then the resulting feeling is bound to be, in many important ways, very dissatisfying. A headlong pursuit of achievement is tough enough; to do so under these restrictions can make for a suffocating combination.

Of course, such parenting does not happen in China alone. As author Michael Lewis has written, "In Japan, mothers insist on achievement and accomplishment as a sign of love and respect. Thus to fail places children in a highly shamed situation." Other cultures promote similar parenting sensibilities. It's not uncommon in South Korea to see kids as young as four or five spending hours and hours hitting golf balls on practice ranges. The belief seems to be that whoever works the hardest and hits the most balls will be the most successful. Making it on the PGA or the LPGA Tour is the pinnacle of success and worth whatever sacrifices might be required, regardless of the age or the wishes of the child.

But it is more than an Asian phenomenon. This parenting style can be found in Canadian hockey, German soccer, Russian tennis, Cuban baseball, and many other arenas. To help young people in the mission they are on, what grand purpose might parents help them to define? For their children to be fulfilled and productive throughout their lives, what attributes might parents help them to establish early on, which will endure? In short, how do parents give children a real sense of value?

The first step—and the most important—is to make sure that your child's scorecard is clear. Does your child know that it's wrong to cheat or show disrespect while in the pursuit of achievement? Does your child know where on the ethical spectrum behaviors like this fall? What about winning and losing—does your child know that winning is not the real end point? For a moment, ponder these questions:

1. Would you rather have your son or daughter cheat and graduate from an Ivy League school or graduate without cheating from a mid-sized metropolitan state college?

2. Do you believe your son or daughter will be happier in life working as a high-profile corporate executive in a well-established firm or as a mid-level manager in a manufacturing plant?

3. Would you rather have your son or daughter lose his or her business or cheat the government out of taxes legitimately owed?

4. Think how excited you became when your son or daughter achieved an important external goal—for example, got an A in math, won the soccer championship, was voted class president or "Most Likely to Succeed." Do you exude the same level of excitement when your child shows strong character traits or acts virtuously?

5. Do you operate under the assumption that the more financially successful your child is, the happier he or she will likely be?

6. Would you like for your child to be well known or even famous?

7. Do you want your child to have many of the material possessions you never had growing up?

8. How much "stuff" does your child have compared to what you had at that age? Is your child happier because of the abundance of possessions?

9. Do you believe that beautiful people are likely to be happier than those who are not? How does your thinking on this impact your child?

10. Which of these "failings" should a child be punished for?
    a. disrespecting others
    b. receiving poor grades
    c. doing something dishonest
    d. failing in math
    e. bullying others
    f. not sharing
    g. flashing a temper
    h. acting arrogantly
    i. acting lazy
    j. losing to a vastly inferior competitor

In brief, given how important it is to us for our kids to achieve, what are we willing to overlook in their lives that perhaps we should not?

PARENTS SEEKING CHILDREN'S APPROVAL

It would not be balanced, or fair, to attack Amy Chua and the parenting style of Tiger Moms (and Tiger Dads) without examining the parenting style on the other end of the spectrum—apparently less rigorous, if more forgiving. There, too, parents may be undermining their children, despite their best intentions. You'd think we would really want to push our kids to achieve goals—and we do—but we also want them, need them, to like us more than maybe any generation of parents has ever wanted this before. "This overly forgiving style probably came up because back in the 1940s and '50s, the grandparents and parents of today's parents were afraid of spoiling their children, so they seldom said anything nice to them," says Dr. Roy Baumeister. "Some of today's parents think back to this and say how they 'never heard anything nice from my mother,' or 'I kept hoping to hear something positive from my father.' This goes back to the Puritan tradition, which obviously was not good. But in correcting this problem, I think we went to the opposite extreme—that parents should always be positive and gushing with their kids. And clearly, that's not good, either." As Carol Dweck writes, "One can hardly walk down the street without hearing parents telling their children how smart they are."

In adopting this counter-Puritan style—running interference for our kids, giving out frequent rewards, and so on—we proceed as if the following were true:

- Possessions have lasting value in terms of stable self-esteem enhancement.
- Using material possessions and money to bribe children into

being virtuous and respectful works. ("I'll buy you a new outfit if you'll start being more respectful of others," "If you don't skip school for the rest of the year I'll buy you a new car.")

- In matters of discipline, being doggedly firm is unnecessary.
- Parents can be too serious about matters of character and virtue.
- Your child will stand firm even if you don't.

By focusing so much on winning the child's goodwill, the parent corrodes the meaning of certain important concepts in the child's mind. Capitulation and rewards are a disastrous way to teach a sense of value. Dr. Baumeister decries "giving everyone a trophy," the culture of rewarding "too often." "This promotion of self-esteem doesn't actually foster healthy self-esteem in kids. It just gives them the message that rewards are meaningless, and they are entitled to be treated well regardless of what they do. That's not a good message to learn and it's not adaptive for life." This message has the undermining effect of creating a serious character malady, says Baumeister. "Problems occur when children are told that they are great no matter what they do—because the parents are afraid that they'll damage their kids' self-esteem if they point out what they did is bad." This is what creates narcissism.

Look at some of the challenges today's parents face, and the very valid reasons why they behave the way they do:

- Parents work long hours, resulting in little time or energy left for disciplining the family.
- Often parents have day care/babysitters/nannies who become surrogate parents. When the parent finally comes home, the last thing he or she wants to do is be negative, no-fun, controlling, overly tough/demanding.
- In an honest attempt to make up for not being there as much as he or she would like, the parent is more permissive and flexible with the child, the better to make the relationship "positive."

- Parents look to children to provide them with emotional support, love, and approval.
- Affluent parents are typically more competitive and connected to material possessions. It's difficult to teach one's own children not to follow one's lead. Researchers Kasser and Ryan have shown that parents who value materialism are more likely to have children who do the same.

Which style works best for kids? The obsessively controlling, overly authoritarian micromanager or the permissive, few-rules-and-expectations best friend? Surely, there are other approaches besides just these two.

"It is easy to get a thousand prescriptions," goes the Chinese proverb, "but hard to get one single remedy."

Amy

Amy, an only child, started playing golf when she was six years old, four years before her parents decided to end their unhappy marriage. Amy's father remarried within the first year of the divorce, but her mom, Sarah, remained single. Because of the divorce settlement, Sarah did not need to work outside the home for both herself and her daughter to live comfortably. By age twelve, Amy started showing extraordinary talent for golf. Hungry to do something meaningful with her life, Sarah decided to manage her daughter's career and proudly stated her mission to me: It was "to do everything I can to help my daughter become a successful playing professional on the LPGA tour." For the next six years, until Amy turned professional, Sarah managed every aspect of Amy's golf life—from practice times to tournament schedules, from what and where to eat to fitness training routines—with extraordinary precision. She traveled with Amy everywhere, attended every practice, workout, and competitive event.

At age seventeen, Amy began to rebel against her mother's

controlling presence. In spite of the escalating turmoil between them, Amy made it through Tour School and earned her LPGA card at the age of nineteen. Sarah brought Amy back to the Institute one month prior to Amy's twentieth birthday because, as she put it, "Amy is becoming a real problem to manage and she has lost her motivation. We've worked so hard to get to this point, but now her work ethic has collapsed. She has a terrible attitude and has lost her self-discipline. The opportunity is right in front of us and she's letting it all slip away. We've got to get her back on track."

After numerous discussions with Amy, her coaches, her fitness trainer, and her agent, we all determined that if Amy was to have any chance of reigniting her love for the game, Sarah would have to give up the controlling role she had held on to for the past seven years. After hearing my recommendation that Amy needed (and wanted) to take ownership and control of her career and that Sarah's involvement was the core problem, Sarah became highly defensive, angry, and attacking. Over the next several weeks of heated discussion and soul-searching, Sarah eventually agreed to let go, to travel only to certain events, and to turn the reins over to her daughter. "I'll do this for Amy," she sighed, "but it seems so unfair. I've devoted the last seven years of my life to get her here, and now when it starts to be fun, I'm asked to bow out?"

Less than two weeks after Sarah relinquished control and returned alone to the family home, she slipped into a very dark, debilitating depression. After barely a month had passed, Sarah called Amy to tell her that life had no meaning for her and that she was seriously considering ending it. Terrified that she might be the reason that serious harm came to her mother, Amy recanted and allowed her mother to resume her role on the team.

Amy continues to struggle with motivation and desire to play on the LPGA tour. She feels trapped with no way out.

ACHIEVEMENT ADDICTION

Children become addicted to achievement just like adults do. I worked not long ago with a teen, Kevin, who suffered from a full-blown addiction to computer games. No matter what Kevin's mother would do (Kevin's father had died two years before), Kevin, like a junkie, would lie and cheat to get his way back onto the computer. Desperate to beat his previous best scores and type in his initials again, he couldn't wait to commemorate his latest and greatest accomplishment—sometimes forgoing sleep and food in the process. Most worrisome of all, when he was deprived of his screen fix for more than twelve to twenty-four hours, he would actually go into a form of withdrawal and walk around in a daze, disengaged and noncommunicative. He was tense, edgy, and defensive. He had no interest in working, earning money, or doing well in school. His desire to relate to other people was completely thwarted. He was living off of the dopamine high of computer game achievement. And the real danger, the reason his "getting clean" fast was so important: The longer the addiction continued, the greater the chance his brain would change the way it functioned. Addiction over time leads to long-term adaptive changes in the brain. The brain is very plastic. As I mentioned earlier, the nucleus accumbens adapts to prolonged addiction, leading to behavioral change, increased sensitization, and further addiction.

The same danger holds for any addiction: not just to drugs, gambling, and sex, but also to fame, materialism, power, and beauty. Living with such an addiction ensures that we are not getting our basic needs met. It means that our happiness, sense of fulfillment, and sense of overall value are being satisfied in a dysfunctional way. The temporarily unhealthy brain chemistry of that condition, if left unchecked, eventually turns into a permanent condition.*

---

* Some may argue that the rewards of obsessive computer game-playing are more intrinsic than extrinsic, but Kevin's greatest sense of reward was the "best score" he got to post when he achieved one.

Take Devin, a sixteen-year-old up-and-coming motocross star, whose recent competitive and medical history includes these dubious hallmarks (so far): four concussions, twenty-five broken bones, and nearly dying in the accident he suffered in his most recent race. In that one, he lost several pints of blood and was initially told he might never walk again. Once he stabilized and doctors upgraded his condition from critical—what was his reaction?

I can't wait to get back on the bike!

The dopamine addiction at work.

Neurophysiologist Wolfram Schultz says that parents can feel the same "high" off of their children's accomplishments as they do off of their own. MRI studies show blood flow increases in dopamine centers of the brain stem when the subject's child achieves.

This finding shouldn't surprise us. Evolutionarily, it makes perfect sense that our children—these creatures who need us for years and years, and to whom we dedicate the bulk of our physical, mental, and emotional resources—should elicit in us this response. It's natural, inevitable.

But it goes deeper than that: Merely *being present* at one's child's competition causes dopamine to be released—they don't even have to succeed! Parents attending practice—where they witness their child achieving new things—becomes a trigger for dopamine release and eventually becomes addictive. As the MRI studies show, the dopamine effect is active even when the subject has *thoughts* of his or her child achieving. Remarkably, the dopamine high from just anticipating what our kids can do is greater than the high from the culmination.

Think of that. Just the thought that your child can outrun a particular person, win the trophy, nail that Chopin étude at the recital, etc., gets your dopamine neurons firing. Put another way, thoughts of our children achieving extrinsic goals evoke in us more or less the same reaction that Pavlov's bell did in his dogs: a physiological response agitating us to satisfy a powerful urge.

It seems clear that such a neurochemical *if-then* can trigger a problematic dynamic, one that inspires some worthwhile questions for parents to ask themselves:

- To what extent am I building my own sense of self-worth through the external achievements of my child? Am I building it, in a sense, on the back of my child?
- If I truly get a "fix" from my child's accomplishments, might I sometimes (though never consciously) favor a short-term goal such as winning, the satisfaction of which is more immediate, over a longer-term goal such as character development, the satisfaction of which is more abstract?
- Is my child feeling added pressure from me to succeed because of the thrill *I* experience when he or she succeeds?
- When my child does not achieve a goal, is my disappointment greater—along with my child's possible sense of devastation—because my dopamine fix has not been satisfied?

WHEN DOES MORAL DEVELOPMENT HAPPEN?

Before getting to the how of your child's moral development, it may be helpful to provide a quick primer on the when. Let us start with Jean Piaget, the Swiss pioneer in cognitive development.

According to Piaget, moral development occurs in response to cognitive changes that are quite predictable. For example, the moral development of six-year-olds, referred to as the Morality of Constraint, is very different from that of twelve-year-olds, called the Morality of Cooperation. Cognitive changes *enable* such moral learning to take place. A typical six-year-old, who believes in Constraint Morality, perceives rules to be established by authority, unchangeable and sacred, and that one should obey these rules because punishment will ensue if one does not. As children grow and develop the cognitive capacity to imagine themselves in place of others (something they lack at a younger age), a shift to Cooperative Morality becomes possible. In this moral stage typical of twelve-year-olds, children obey rules for a new reason: concern for the rights of others. The child is capable of judging others by their intentions rather than by simple consequences; the child can also show respect for the opinions of others while at the same time valuing his or her own thoughts and ideas.

In the late 1950s, several decades after Piaget developed his theory, psychologist Lawrence Kohlberg expanded Piaget's thinking to include three levels of moral reasoning, each made up of two stages, "each more adequate at responding to moral dilemmas than its predecessor." The first level, Pre-Conventional, consists of Obedience and Punishment (Stage 1) and Self-Interest (Stage 2). Thus, elementary school children obey because they are told to do so by an authority figure and will receive punishment if they violate the rule (Stage 1) and because they are acting in their own best interest (Stage 2).

Kohlberg's second level of moral reasoning, Conventional, consists of Social Norms (Stage 3, in which moral decisions are based on the approval of others) and Authority and Social Order (Stage 4, in which moral decisions are made by abiding with established law and fulfilling the obligation of duty).

Kohlberg's third level, Post-Conventional, consists of Social Contract (Stage 5) and Principled Conscience (Stage 6).

According to Kohlberg's findings, most adults, sad though it is, fail to reach this third level of moral thinking—either Stage 5, which is based on a sincere interest in the welfare of others and a sense of social mutuality, or Stage 6, the final and most evolved state, where moral reasoning is based on respect for universal principles and individual conscience.

Kohlberg believed strongly that stages of moral development could not be bypassed: One must master specific developmental lessons before moving on to those of the next, higher stage. He felt strongly, too, that one of the best ways to stimulate moral development was through teaching—by presenting moral dilemmas for discussion. Like Piaget, Kohlberg was convinced that moral development occurs through social interaction.

Kohlberg's work has been studied and discussed extensively. Some of his stages have been confirmed by the research community and some have not. Some critics suggest that he focused too much on the value of justice, to the exclusion of other values. Psychologist Carol Gilligan argued that his theory focused too heavily on male subjects (initially he used only male participants in his research). Whatever its arguable shortcomings, though, his work, and Piaget's, demonstrated that *there is a clear developmental learning process to becoming a moral person*. Kohlberg further built on Piaget's work by asserting that moral development continued throughout one's life.

Although both models provide important insights, perhaps the most useful model is a third one—by psychologist Erik Erikson, the first person specifically to link developmental stages with character and virtues.

Erikson's Eight-Stage Model of Moral Development

Erikson's moral development model is particularly important because of its classification of character strengths based on insights he gained through his research. Each of Erikson's chronological stages have corresponding character strengths. Usefully, his model also provides age-specific guidelines for learning virtues and demonstrates how the learning and non-learning of specific virtues has a developmental trajectory.

ERIKSON'S EIGHT-STAGE MODEL

STAGE	APPROXIMATE AGES	CHARACTER STRENGTH/VIRTUE
I	birth to 1	hope, faith
II	age 1 to 3	will, determination
III	age 3 to 6	purpose, courage

(Continued)

STAGE	APPROXIMATE AGES	CHARACTER STRENGTH/VIRTUE
IV	age 6 to puberty	competence
V	puberty to age 18	fidelity, loyalty
VI	age 18 to 25	love
VII	age 25 to 50	care
VIII	age 50 to death	wisdom

Erikson's model is fundamentally aligned with Self-Determination Theory, so widely accepted by researchers today. Indeed, Erikson's Stages II through IV speak to the three needs—for autonomy, relatedness, and mastery—that SDT asserts are most fundamental to our well-being.

Like Piaget before him and Kohlberg after, Erikson saw moral development as a step-by-step process: When we learn virtues at the suitable developmental time, the door opens to the next set of virtues, appropriate for the next developmental stage. Miss one of those stages and a critical door of moral development can and will close. If that happens, a variety of psychosocial crises in adulthood can impede further moral development. For example: When an infant's need for trust is not fulfilled in Stage I, he may experience pervasive mistrust of others throughout adulthood. When a child's need for autonomy is not met in Stage II, she may start to feel shame and doubt, which often results in impulsive/compulsive behavior in adulthood. When a child's need for purpose is not satisfied in Stage III, he may grow to be a ruthless, uninhibited adult. When a teen's need for loyalty and fidelity are not met in Stage V, she may be prone to fanaticism and role confusion later in life. When a young adult's needs for love and care are thwarted in Stages VI and VII, his capacity for intimacy and connection to others may be seriously compromised, resulting in excessive self-absorption throughout life. In Erikson's final state, despair becomes the steep psychosocial price one pays for one's needs not being adequately fulfilled.

Erikson was convinced that when a stage was satisfactorily "passed," the character strengths and virtues spawned by that stage facilitated the emergence of the next stage. In their book, *Character Strengths and Virtues*, Christopher Peterson and Martin Seligman created the following chart illuminating the connection between Erikson's eight stages and the resulting character development.

APPROXIMATE AGES	CHARACTERIZATION	RESULTING CHARACTER STRENGTH
birth to age 1	Infants must learn to achieve a sense of safety, trusting caretakers to provide for their well-being.	Trust (hope, gratitude)
age 1 to age 3	Children must learn to make things happen, to choose, to exercise will.	Autonomy (persistence)
age 3 to age 6	Children must learn to initiate their own activities, thereby gaining confidence in oneself.	Initiative (curiosity)
age 6 to puberty	Children must learn to explore systematically their skills and abilities.	Competence (love of learning; creativity)
puberty to age 18	Adolescents must create a set of personal values and goals by which to live, represented as a coherent identity.	Identity (social intelligence; spirituality)
age 18 to age 25	Young adults must learn to merge their identity with that of another person.	Intimacy (love)
age 25 to age 50	Middle-aged adults must learn to concern themselves with the world and the next generation.	Generativity (kindness)
age 50 to death	Later adults must come to terms with how they have resolved previous issues.	Ego integrity (integrity; perspective)

This history of moral development is by no means exhaustive (Erikson would later come up with a ninth stage; Kohlberg, a seventh). But it provides, I hope, an adequate framework for the recommendations to follow.

WHY PARENTS CARRY THE GREATEST RESPONSIBILITY

The responsibility for character development is determined by access: Who has the most time to influence the child? From birth through age six, the responsibility for character development falls to parents, with grandparents often providing important assistance. From ages seven to eighteen, the responsibility is shared by parents (foremost still) along with teachers, coaches, and administrators. From age nineteen and on, the prime responsibility falls to the individual, with the larger community providing additional support where possible. Although most of the critical inputs are made before adolescence, character growth and development ought to continue throughout one's lifetime.

Character is formed by building habits: habits of doing, feeling, thinking, judging. Saying "thank you," letting others go first, being courteous and polite, speaking the truth, showing compassion, being respectful or humble, etc.—these become habitual through repeated practice.

When teaching character-based lessons to children, how do parents get them to embrace respect for others, to understand integrity and compassion and justice? How early can a child understand these concepts?

Here are some guidelines, with eyes fixed on developing strong character.

What Parents Can Do to Help Kids Build Character

1. Make the character development of your children your highest priority every day, every month, every year. If there is one parenting thing to obsess over, make it this: having your child possess the finest moral character possible—not getting into Stanford, or being the star quarterback, or developing superior moneymaking skills. This is the essence of character building for parents.

2. Create your own character-based scorecard and talk about it regularly, especially when teachable moments arise. Share it with your children as soon as their cognitive, intellectual, and moral development allows comprehension. By age seven, primitive understandings of right and wrong, effort, attitude, obedience, fairness, etc., allow for many character scorecard concepts to be explored and taught. Other concepts—such as loyalty, caring, and empathy—will need to wait until the child is older.

3. Help your children develop their own character-based scorecards, and use them daily or weekly; this ensures that issues of character get top billing in their lives. Put their scorecard on the refrigerator. Put your own there, as well. The child grades his or her scorecard, and the parents grade their own. This helps instill the primacy of the scorecard, promotes accountability, helps to establish that character is a dominant part of one's identity, and makes character development real. At the Institute, children as young as nine who attend our tennis academy must, as part of their attendance, create their own character scorecard and grade themselves regularly. Coaches also review and grade the kids' scorecards. Athletes are encouraged to select a specific character trait or virtue to be exercised through intentional energy investment each week. Our coaches are frequently astonished at the positive impact this practice has on the behavior of kids both on and off the court. Some of these remarkable examples appear in Chapter 9.

4. Never use your children's accomplishments to build your own self-esteem. As Matt Davidson, president and director of

education for the Institute for Excellence and Ethics (IEE), wrote, "Don't see [your children] as a scholarship. Don't use them to achieve your hopes and dreams—past or future. Don't play them as pawns in your game of social climbing and competition. Love them—with their unique personalities and temperaments, with their unique talents and abilities, and with all their unique character strengths *and* weaknesses."

5. Your sense of value should come from the same place as your child's: alignment of one's life with core character strengths.

6. Praise energy invested over outcome every time. "Failure syndrome," as Carol Dweck has taught us, comes from unearned self-esteem. Kids are lavished with unmerited praise, which turns out to be the flimsy foundation for a (false) sense of self that collapses at the first sign of failure. Telling children they are the greatest, most talented, prettiest, etc., in an effort to build confidence and self-esteem has, all too often, the precise opposite effect. But when you praise a child for investing his or her best energy (focused, positive, fully committed, etc.), it is more genuinely rewarding. Why? Because the child has control over it.

7. Make your love unconditional. For a parent, unconditional love means caring for your child without qualification. Your child doesn't have to earn your deep parental caring and affection. You will still love your child whether or not your child acts ethically, respectfully, truthfully, or graciously. You will not, however, *overlook* character deficiencies or collapses. Self-esteem should always be earned, but parental love should be unconditional—always.

8. Continually reinforce the message to your children that their character will be built from the choices they make on a daily basis. Every choice they make has character consequences. No one can build their character but themselves.

9. Help your children to understand that the "muscles" of character are built and maintained in the same way that muscles of the

body are: by regular energy investment. Teach them concretely how this can be done in their lives.

10. As a parent, model the character traits you want your children to learn. Be the desired virtue yourself: kind, faithful, loving, grateful, courageous, etc.

11. Ensure that your children are socially connected and engaged at home and in school. Character does not grow in isolation or disconnection from others. Our fundamental need for relatedness is so deeply ingrained in who we are as human beings that absent such connection, healthy character development simply cannot occur.

12. Assignment: Everyone in the family has to perform acts of kindness and report back on them. Sonja Lyubomirsky has discovered the benefit that comes from doing all of your acts of kindness in the same day, as opposed to spreading them out over a week's time. The impact on well-being is far greater.

13. Use winning and losing in sport as special opportunities to teach lessons about character, intrinsic vs. extrinsic success, achievement, etc.

14. Use every crisis and critical decision in your child's life to teach moral reasoning and good judgment. Encourage your child to refer to his or her Ultimate Mission and character scorecard before making any important decision. In *Character Matters*, Thomas Lickona recommends that the child ask himself or herself the following nine questions to determine if a decision or action passes the ethical test:
    - Would I want people to do this to me?
    - Is this fair to everybody who might be affected by what I do or say?
    - Would I like it if everyone else did this?
    - Does this action represent the whole truth and nothing but the truth?
    - How would my parents feel if they found out I did this?

- Does this go against my religion?
- Does this go against my conscience?
- Might this have bad consequences?
- How would I feel if my action were reported on the front page of my hometown paper?

Developing character competence in kids is more important, I contend, than developing their emotional or intellectual competence. IQ is important; EQ (emotional quotient) is important; CQ (character quotient) trumps them both, without question. Parents must make character, most importantly ethical character, the number one consideration in everything they do with their children.

And there are only so many days before life's tests start cascading down on children. Nothing good comes from delaying the countdown. Everyone who plays a role in building a child's character formulation—parents, grandparents, teachers, coaches, administrators, employers—must rally to the cause of urgency.

How many days does one get to help guide a child's character development?

The race is on.

What Teachers Can Do to Help Kids Build Character

1. Have students write character-related essays on issues such as "What is character and why does it matter?"; "Character is destiny"; "Moral intelligence in action"; "Character strengths I most want to embody"; "How is character formed?"
2. Find ways to relate what a child learns in class—be it in social studies, math, history, science, physical education, etc.—with issues of performance character and moral character. Highlight the character strengths and flaws of great thinkers, leaders, contributors, artists, and historical figures.
3. Bring former students into the classroom to speak about the importance of character and ethics. Have them give concrete

examples from their own lives that underscore the critical role character plays in navigating life's storms.

4. Hang a "Character Strength of the Month" poster in a prominent place in the classroom. Encourage students to find examples from newspapers, magazines, and various life experiences that relate to the character theme in question. Papers, essays, speeches, skits, etc., can all be themed around a particular character trait or virtue for the month.

5. Give students an opportunity on a regular basis to ponder challenging questions such as "What is happiness and where does it come from?"; "What gives your life meaning and purpose?"; "How do you want to be remembered at the end of your life?"; "What criteria will you use to determine the success or failure of your life?"

6. Make an array of community service opportunities available to students and connect their experiences with these to issues of character development.

7. Use tragic current events to focus on character learning. War, human-made disasters, corporate scandals, sport scandals, crime, political corruption, etc., provide vivid, real-life opportunities to address why character formation is so important.

8. Help students to understand how homework may be used to acquire important performance character strengths such as perseverance, time management, self-discipline, concentration, and full engagement. This provides a deeper sense of purpose for homework—a particularly worthwhile pursuit for the student, to whom homework often appears to have little or no practical value.

9. Give anonymous, weekly character compliments to one student nominated by the teacher. From a list of performance and moral character traits, students anonymously compliment a fellow student for displaying or possessing certain character traits. The feedback given the designated student catalyzes positive character development: The student focuses on it, invests more energy in it, strengthens it.

10. Educate students each week on the practical value of a particular character trait or virtue. For example: Teach them that fortitude is considered by some to be "the great virtue" because it mobilizes the courage necessary to follow our purpose in life; it provides the will to do right when the tide is pushing hard in the opposite direction. Without fortitude, we would surrender, and quickly, to the forces of the dark side. Another example would be helping your children understand how doing what one says one will do is an important aspect of integrity.

What Coaches Can Do to Help Kids Build Character

1. Establish character development to be the number one objective in your coaching. Just as John Wooden did, let your athletes know the scorecard you use to define success in your coaching career. Let their parents know, too.

2. In every practice and every game, reference the character traits and virtues you expect your players to invest in. Some of these will be performance character strengths, some moral character strengths.

3. Make sure that matters of character supersede matters of winning in all your interactions with players, parents, and fellow coaches—before, during, and after games.

4. The book *Whose Game Is It, Anyway?*, by Amy Baltzell, Richard D. Ginsburg, and Stephen Durant, is written from three perspectives: the athlete's, the parents', and the coach's. It advocates that every important decision ought to be made with those three stakeholders in mind. This may not always be practical, but it's worth examining how many of the decisions you make might be usefully expanded to include other important perspectives. According to the authors, for kids to develop strong character through sport "coaches must provide accurate praise and positive reinforcement, not just for good plays or successful outcomes but also for virtuous behavior." Never use the external achievements

of your athletes to build your own self-esteem or sense of personal value, and never allow your players to judge their self-worth by the number of wins or losses they accumulate during the season. Constantly emphasize values such as trust, loyalty, hard work, commitment, and respect for each member of the team and for opponents. Talk regularly about ethical values and make these values come to life every day in practice.

5. Set firm limits regarding moral violations for everyone. Make sure star players are granted no special privileges if and when they've committed failures of ethical character.

No one is born with strong character. It can and must be taught. In some cases, the students are children, and parents are responsible for teaching these lessons. However, in other cases teachers, coaches, and managers must take on the challenge when parents are unwilling or unable to do so. Regardless of the audience, this chapter has outlined concrete steps business leaders, parents, teachers, and coaches can take to accelerate this essential learning process. The payoff is priceless.

PART IV

Back to Chasing Achievement Again—with the New Scorecard

9

Getting Your Story Straight About Achievement

Talents are best nurtured in solitude. Character is best formed
in the stormy billows of the world.

—GOETHE

Remember Scott, the CEO millionaire who, on the very first page of the Introduction to this book, sat across from me, daze and confused?

His salary is still north of a million dollars; he still owns three homes, still never flies commercial; and his company has about the same number of employees. Those things haven't changed in the nine months since Scott first attended our two-and-a-half-day Executive Course. Some things, however, have changed, and significantly, according to 360-degree feedback from Scott's direct reports, his wife Sherri, his two teenage sons, and from Scott himself. The most significant changes at work, according to his work reports, have been emotional and spiritual. The biggest gains emotionally were jumps in gratitude (3.6 to 5.2 on a 7-point scale), compassion (3.9 to 5.5), warmth and caring (3.3 to 4.4), and expressing more joy and satisfaction (3.1 to 4.0).

According to Sherri and his two sons, Scott is more devoted, more engaged, and more present in their lives. Both sons perceive their father to be more patient with them, less stubborn, and more focused when they are together. Sherri wrote the following in her 360-degree report:

> *I love what's happened to Scott. He's a very different person at home. His priorities have clearly shifted when it comes to his family. He's also happier and more fun to be around. Even after 21 years of marriage, I feel closer to him than ever. I pray the changes will last.*

According to Scott's 360 results, he has made significant gains in the area of his spiritual alignment: To the statement, "the energy I give to my family is consistent with how much I value them," he jumped from 2.8 to 5.1; to "the decision and behaviors I engage in each day reflect what I value most in my life," he jumped from 3.0 to 5.0; and to "what I say to others and myself is a reflection of my purpose," he jumped from 3.1 to 4.6. In Scott's own words, "I'm more purpose-driven in everything I do. I'm clear on the legacy I want to leave behind—I want to be remembered most for my devotion to my family and for my strong character. I've got much more ground to cover but I'm definitely getting better. I'm also much happier and at peace with myself." The second round of testing data was collected when Scott brought his fourteen direct reports to the Institute, roughly nine months after his initial visit.

RE-PURPOSING EXTRINSIC ACHIEVEMENT

You've learned the importance of determining your grand purpose in life and ways to help you define and refine it. You've also learned how to construct a scorecard for the achievement of that grand purpose, something we refer to in our training as your Ultimate Mission. Finally, you've learned that character development is the targeted endpoint for every external achievement you pursue.

One more thing—*Achievement is indispensable.*

The ideas underpinning this book are not "anti-achievement" or "anti-competition," though at times it may appear that way. Achievement is as vital under the new scorecard as it was under the old. We must advance toward a desired goal. Without it, neither meaningful challenge nor accountability is possible. Without it—to return to the muscle-building metaphor—there is insufficient stress exposure to stimulate growth. Put simply, accelerated growth requires a chase.

The key distinction between your scorecard and society's, a distinction I hope is clear by now, is that not all achievement is equal. The new scorecard, the *character scorecard*, changes what was previously meant by purpose. Up to now, success has largely been defined by the size of the victory or prize itself, no matter how it was achieved or at what cost. The end *was* the purpose, and the end justified the means (including doing whatever it took to achieve it).

My years of work with superachievers has helped me understand that feeling successful cannot be assumed just because one has achieved something. The underlying purpose and cost must be plumbed: Want to climb Everest? Okay—but that means leaving your family for an extended period of time. Is that justified according to your deepest values? What is your real purpose for climbing? This same questions were asked in Chapter 1, only now you have a template to better judge the rightness or wrongness of your answers—your Ultimate Mission and your resulting character scorecard. So let's explore the questions again: Are you climbing the mountain to cross off one more thing on your bucket list before you die? Is it because you're a goal-oriented person and what better goal is there than climbing Everest? Do you do it to show you're a successful person? Do you do it to satisfy your unquenchable thirst for visible achievement? Is the whole endeavor likely to give life to things about yourself that you already don't like—say, self-absorption and hubris? Or, on the other hand, is this chase to climb Mount Everest truly going to help you meet your basic needs: for autonomy, mastery, and especially relatedness? Is training for the climb and then the actual climb itself going to make you increasingly better at being the person you want to be? Are the gains more about what you are doing for others (relatedness) or more about you? If it's the latter, then how much lasting value can actually be packed into the endeavor, if virtue and value are most always centered on others?

Sir Edmund Hillary publically criticized New Zealander Mark Inglis and forty other climbers who, in various groups, left British climber David Sharp to die in May 2006. Said Sir Hillary, "I think the whole attitude towards climbing Mount Everest has become rather horrifying. . . . People just want to get to the top, they don't give a damn for anybody else who may be in distress, and it doesn't impress me at all that they leave someone lying under a rock to die."

Suppose you achieve the extrinsic objective—say you reach the very top of Everest, or get as close as humanly possible under the circumstances—but in so doing, you ignore an important ethical value and place people you care most about at serious risk. In less spectacular but no less powerful ways, this Everest example eerily mirrors what has been happening for years and years to so many of the businessmen and -women who find themselves sitting in our workshops, head in hands, or wearing a look halfway between daze and shock, as they confront the reality that important beliefs have been compromised. Their life lacks value because they have spent upward of 90 percent of it chasing things empty of sustainable meaning. In their sanest moment, upon serious reflection, they admit that they are not very happy with who they have become as a consequence of their pursuit of extrinsic success. Even those few who meet all the extrinsic markers of success but did so at the expense of intrinsic growth find themselves struggling with a painful sense of hollowness and disillusionment. Tragically, without the right purpose, they fail whether they achieve or don't achieve.

It's important to understand that although extrinsic achievement is not the end point, it is clearly not discouraged. Its value is simply redefined and kept in perspective. You use the forces and stresses of everything you chase *extrinsically* to help become everything you want and need to become *intrinsically*.

So, yes: The pursuit of extrinsic achievement in the service of intrinsic growth can be undertaken in the crucible of our typically high-demand, high-stress lives; indeed such an environment can help to facilitate growth. The more you push and the more resistance you encounter, the richer the opportunity to build and grow the fundamental values and virtues you hold most dear. You're always adjusting, refining, balancing to nourish the capacities you cherish most, particularly when the going is toughest.

STORMS ARE THE TRAINING GROUND FOR CHARACTER

Character traits cannot be built in a vacuum. They must be steadily challenged to grow. "The weakest of all weak things is a virtue which has not been tested in the fire," wrote Mark Twain.

That's where storms come in. Storms are simply life challenges that push us outside our comfort zone. We *need* storms because they demand energy investments—physical, emotional, mental, and spiritual. Storms bring us face-to-face with our fears, our values, our sense of right and wrong, our moral compass. Every storm is both a character test and a character-building opportunity. Absent the stress of the storm, character strength neither grows nor is revealed. "Things that appear to be obstacles turn out to be desirable in the long haul," says Professor Robert Bjork, chairman of the UCLA psychology department. He is by no means the first or only person to suggest that when things get harder, or when you make them harder on yourself, learning accelerates.

Martin Seligman first made his mark by identifying the notion of "learned helplessness," which argues that people (though it was first discovered in animals) behave helplessly in situations even when their ability to improve the outcome exists. In a later book, called *Learned Optimism*, he delineated a fundamental difference: There are people who can experience repeated failures and somehow never quit, and people who will give up. For the former, "optimistic" group, setbacks are viewed as temporary. Seligman suggested that the centerpost in a healthy person's life is the capacity for optimism, which opens the door for hope; without hope, there is no fight, much less growth. We tend to thrive when we see opportunities for growth, not when we are in defensive mode. People who are truly healthy and resilient fight through life's storms, fight through depression, strengthening and using, along the way, both performance character muscles (perseverance, self-discipline, courage, etc.) as well as moral character muscles (humility, caring, gratitude, etc.).

In her excellent book *Positivity*, researcher Barbara Fredrickson presents, in a similar way, considerable scientific evidence supporting the importance of maintaining a positive mind-set in navigating through the storms of life. "Positivity transforms us for the better," she argues. "By opening our hearts and minds, positive emotions allow us to discover and build new skills, new ties, new knowledge, and new ways of being."

Perhaps no one grasps this idea—personally and professionally, intellectually and emotionally—better than Viktor Frankl, the late, great Austrian psychiatrist and Holocaust survivor, who spent two and a half years at the Theresienstadt concentration camp, at Auschwitz, and at Turkheim (affiliated with Dachau). His wife was murdered at the Bergen-Belsen camp, his mother at Auschwitz, and his father died while at Theresienstadt.

In his book *Man's Search for Meaning*, Frankl wrote about the amazing ability of human beings to create a sense of meaning and purpose out of even the most wretched, dehumanizing environments. It is both comforting and inspiring for us to witness his penetrating insights. As someone who had been through the Holocaust, Frankl had every justification to turn cynical about humankind. But he concluded that even suffering itself can be used to fuel meaningful achievement and growth. No matter what you're exposed to, no matter what turbulence you're experiencing, ask yourself these questions: *What is valuable here? Who do I want to be, consistent with my deepest values, in this environment? How can I continue to move toward my ultimate purpose? Amid the chaos, where should I be focusing my energy? What choices do I still have?*

Rita

Rita is a waitress, a single mom with two young daughters, trying to make ends meet. What does she value most? She wants to be a great loving and caring mother. She wants to give her best energy to her daughters when she's with them, which from her perspective doesn't happen nearly enough. She wants not only to convey a sense of warmth, caring, and respect for them, but to embody these traits in her own life, so that her children understand what strength actually looks like in real terms. Warm, caring, respectful of others, engaged—these are some of the character strengths she has listed on her scorecard. But how will she nurture these amid the stress of her busy, overworked life? All too often her customers don't deserve respect, nor do some of her colleagues, and certainly not her boss. In fact, the restaurant where she works is a pretty brutal environment. There is no shortage of opportunities for her to become jaded, sarcastic, perfunctory, dismissive.

But however bad things get, she knows, via her scorecard and the hard work that went into building it, that she wants to be a person of compassion, warmth, respect, and optimism. It will not be satisfying to her, and certainly not to her daughters, if she is cynical, self-absorbed, cold, disengaged, and bitter. To find happiness, she needs to grow intrinsically, even in difficult circumstances.

"The test of a well-functioning conscience," wrote Polly Young-Eisendrath in *The Self-Esteem Trap*, "means having the character and courage to do the right thing *even if it costs more than you want to pay* [emphasis added]. In fact conscience isn't entirely real until it's tested. Until then it's a set of ideals, or worse, something that is given lip service for the sake of appearance." Dr. Young-Eisendrath could have written those sentences about just about any virtue—patience, endurance, generosity, you name it. As for our single mom, one day she won't be waiting on her nasty customers or working for a tyrannical boss. Perhaps Rita will be promoted to manager. Or have a different job. Or she'll still be a waitress but will have enhanced her capacity to deal with what she has to deal with now. If she keeps going back to her scorecard, and honing those character traits, then she will continue to grow as a person regardless of her environment. Whatever storm she faces in her life, her scorecard is her lighthouse. It allows her to see home always—to turn inward to things that are accessible, rather than looking to the often out-of-control, sometimes hostile outside world, where she could easily feel helpless and without options.

But of course she *does* have options. She does have control, control of where she invests her energy and what she invests it in. Things of the utmost value *can* be nourished. She can always get kinder, can always become more honest, more respectful, more grateful, and more self-disciplined. If she continues to walk that path, she will not lose her hard-won sense of value. Society may not value her intrinsic pursuit of character strengths as much as it values other pursuits and successes, but this is where true happiness and fulfillment are born and can never be stolen from her. As we so often witness, people who have the most of what society admires are very often the least happy.

EVERYTHING IS AN OPPORTUNITY TO GROW CHARACTER—EVERYTHING

While it is true that, though intensely painful, events of greatest adversity also give us the greatest opportunity to build character, it is also true that everything, every single day, can be used to build character strengths. Sport, work, family life, even downtime—all can be employed to leverage character improvement. Mistakes on the tennis or basketball court, or failures in the boardroom or in one's leadership create the channel, if managed properly, for one to become more of the idealized person one wishes to become. They allow one to grow in whatever strengths one aspires to emulate. And such character development can never start too young. Our Human Performance Institute junior tennis program, under the tutelage of teacher-coach Lorenzo Beltrame, has been developed specifically so that our young athletes intentionally use their tennis experience as a character-building vehicle. The program was purposely designed, first and foremost, to meet our athletes' basic needs as outlined in Deci and Ryan's Self-Determination Theory:

1. *Need for autonomy*: Our kids are given as many choices as possible regarding their tennis—why they want to play, how far they want to go, what tournaments they want to play, whether they want to play at all. They also get to choose which character strengths they wish to acquire as they chase tennis success. Being forced to participate because "it will be good for you" serves only to smother the need for autonomy and promotes burnout.

2. *Need for competency and mastery*: Everything is done to encourage our kids to find great joy and fulfillment in learning, in getting better, in the simple act of hitting balls for its own sake. Our goal is to help them understand the deep sense of fulfillment they can derive from simply acquiring mastery of something very difficult.

3. *Need for relatedness*: This is where moral character strengths come in. At least half of our students' scorecard entries must be from the moral character list. The moral/ethical traits are always given highest priority—respect for others, caring for others, kindness, integrity, and trust.

Our players are coached to use winning, losing, and the demands of tennis to become extraordinary people. They work very hard every day at tennis to become the people they want to be, to grow the muscles that will one day define their greatest assets. Our hope is that the pursuit of tennis in this special way will serve as a template for them throughout their lives, providing guidance in how and why to pursue anything and everything. The hope is that this will enable them to live lives of great value to the end, without regrets.

So much of what the kids learn at the Human Performance Institute Tennis Academy is filtered through what happens on the court. When they lose, they know they have more to learn. They also know that winning too much can arouse an exaggerated view of oneself, a sense of superiority, even an invincibility that is unrealistic and damaging. We want our players to be challenged seriously but still win more than half the time, if possible. When they lose, the internal learning is typically richer and deeper, each loss a chance to build resiliency, persistence, perspective, and dedication.

Our young players see that growth happening in themselves and in their teammates in very tangible ways.

WHAT ARE THE RESULTS?

Our student-athletes have a love affair with tennis—unlike, I'm sad to say, far too many children and teens in other elite junior training programs. Our kids love tennis because they see it for what it is—a fabulous opportunity to grow up and to build physical, emotional, mental, and spiritual strength. So if they never make it to the top of professional tennis, they will still value all the hard work and sacrifices they have invested because, most importantly, it helped them build their inner core of life strengths.

Some actual examples of athletes at our academy, ranging in age from nine to eighteen, whose investment in sport is linked to a purpose beyond winning and beyond themselves:

- *Efren, age fifteen*: "When I grow up I want to be enthusiastic, to smile and be positive. I also want to believe in myself. That's one of the most important reasons I play tennis."
- *Sid, age sixteen*: "Tennis helps me give my full attention to whatever task lies in front of me. I will be able to achieve the many

things that I want to accomplish using the training mind-set I've learned through the hard work of tennis. I want to be someone that brings light to a dull place and tennis is helping me do that."

- *Killian, age fifteen*: "My highest goal for tennis this year is to improve on my self-control. Self-control is very important not only on the tennis court but also outside of tennis in my life overall. For me, having self-control means having integrity and keeping every promise I make to others and to myself. This is important because it connects to many other traits such as honesty, respect, and gratefulness. My self-control affects other people."

- *Alom, age fifteen*: "I use tennis to help me in life later on by framing every match, every practice as an opportunity to improve upon myself. After falling, I get back up, and during a good moment, I try and get the most out of what is going on. In school I am able to get good grades without studying every night. Tennis forces me to push my limits and work harder than I do in all other aspects in my life. I look for the little victories, such as giving my best effort and keeping calm under pressure."

- *Sharon, age fourteen*: "I use tennis to help me become the person I want to be. Every day of tennis I see as a test of my character and an opportunity to become a stronger person. For me, tennis is not so much about wins and losses, but what's happening inside me because of them."

At HPI, the coaching certification program we run annually attracts dozens of the top athletic coaches from around the world; our core philosophy is that coaches are at their best when helping kids realize who they want to be as human beings, then using the sport to help their young athletes build toward that. We start the program by asking the coaches who *they* want to be and the legacy they want to leave behind. The answer, it turns out, never has anything to do with the number of NCAA titles won. No matter how "successful" the coaches have been—and we've hosted many of the highest-profile practitioners across practically every major sport—those who have been through the program invariably say some version of "What I really want is to help these young men/women to become better human beings." Jeremy Foley, athletic director at the University of Florida, told me, "I want a program that builds kids with character." He is not alone.

WINNING WITH CHARACTER

Goals that seemed unattainable under the old scorecard are reachable under the new one. Let me explain what I mean.

For decades, legions of coaches, athletes, and parents have held the belief that nice, warm, sensitive, caring, respectful, kind people make lousy competitors. "To be a great competitor, you need to have the heart of an assassin," a highly successful coach once told me. "The more I can get my players to hate their opponents, to see them as evil people deserving to be punished, it stirs the good stuff in their blood and I get more out of them. When the game is really big, I'll demonize the opposing team and it raises the fight in my guys." The implication is that to become a great competitor, one must jettison a host of moral character traits such as respect for one's opponent, including kindness and compassion.

I might point out that in just the last year, the junior players referenced in the previous section—the ones who are each making profound leaps in ethical and performance character every time they step on the tennis court—have, collectively, won twenty-three junior tennis titles, been finalists in six events, semifinalists in three, quarterfinalists in five.

But lest that sample be dismissed as selective or not applicable, let me go right to the absolute top of the sport. There, one finds a shining example that character need not be sacrificed at the altar of traditional competitive "success": the rivalry between Roger Federer of Switzerland and Rafael Nadal of Spain.

This rivalry pits against each other two of the greatest players the game has ever seen. Federer held the ATP number one world ranking for 237 consecutive weeks, won a male record sixteen Grand Slam singles titles, appeared in an unprecedented twenty-two career Grand Slam finals, and won Olympic gold at the 2008 Summer Olympic Games. Many current and former players consider Federer the greatest player of all time.

Nadal, widely hailed as history's greatest clay-court player, has won ten Grand Slam titles, Olympic gold, and is the youngest player of the Open era to complete the career Grand Slam. He has won a record nineteen ATP World Tour Masters titles. And he's almost five years younger than Federer.

Rivalries in tennis, like those in boxing, can become bigger than life; they can, and frequently do, become contentious, even nasty. The old myth was that fierce rivals could never be friendly (much less friends), enjoy each other's company, or even have respect for each other; to do so would be to destroy the competitive fire needed to kick the other one's butt. Jimmy Connors, the fiery champion of the 1970s and '80s, was coached and managed by his mother, who felt as if each match her son played was a war. Jimmy could never really enjoy the friendship of someone he wanted to beat. In the NFL (and other sports and leagues, as well), it has often been frowned on to chat with opponents even when the game is done.

Because they play in the same era, Federer and Nadal provide us with an almost perfect storm of conditions, to see if this notion is true or mostly rubbish. The two men share a level of individual greatness, have enjoyed a similar level of success (though Federer has been doing it for a few more years), and a similar competitive fire. As historical sports rivals go, it doesn't get juicier than Federer-Nadal. They have faced each other in eight Grand Slam finals, with Nadal winning six, battled in ten other finals and six non-finals—twenty-four matches in all. Their 2008 Wimbledon final is considered by many experts to be the greatest match in tennis history.

So let's look at the rivalry from the perspective of the character scorecard. Neither of their checklists seems consistent with that of "an assassin":

CHARACTER STRENGTH	FEDERER	NADAL
Respect for opponent	A	A
Humility	A	A
No trash talking	A	A
Compassion for opponent in victory	A	A
No excuse-making in defeat	A	A

It's worth noting that Federer and Nadal did not earn their straight A's simply by deciding one day to be virtuous in this way or that. They, like all of us, had to work at it, continually. Respect for the opponent is a character strength they fine-tuned over many, many matches across many years and hone with each competition— even in the fiercest battles with each other, in Grand Slam finals that obviously mean a great deal to both men. And their mutual respect has positive effects beyond just them. Early on, word of it spread around the pro tennis locker room, an example to others. At least as importantly, theirs is an example for young players and fans, too. Whether or not there are reasons—spreading a message of character, being a good role model, etc.—that Federer and Nadal act this way, I can't say. But it's clear that by comporting themselves just so, they are doing something steeped in "relatedness" and fulfilling a purpose larger than themselves. They make us all proud.

What's more, "character wins"—unlike tournament wins—are never at the expense of someone else: When Nadal or Federer gets an A for respecting his opponent or being humble, it doesn't deprive his rival or anyone else of also earning A's in that category. For intrinsic achievement, we are being judged only and always against our own scorecard (be it explicit or not), thus there is a boundless amount of victory possible—not true for the extrinsic variety. In his short story "The Man That Corrupted Hadleyburg," Mark Twain mocks the notion that there is only so much good character to go around; in the locale of the title, various townspeople try fruitlessly to "out-virtue" one another.

My intimate, decades-long involvement in professional tennis has provided me with a long list of current and former professional tennis players who bust the myth that champions need to be jerks, that external success must somehow go hand in hand with character deficit: Kim Clijsters, winner of four Grand Slam titles; Bob and Mike Bryan, the greatest doubles team in tennis history; Maria Sharapova; Monica Seles; Patrick Rafter; Todd Martin; and Tom and Tim Gullikson, to mention just a very few. Dan Jansen not only won Olympic gold and multiple world speed skating championships, dominating his event for years, but did so in a way that was admirably humble: Early on he learned "to thank the timer, the volunteers, the backup timer who were out there every week, standing in the cold. My parents were proud of the things I did on the ice but it was equally important that I showed respect to the people who enabled me to do it."

Society's Scorecard has made sports competition an arena where athletes are allowed, even encouraged, to show arrogance and ego, to resent and openly despise authority figures, referees, and opponents, as ways of gaining the necessary edge. But it does not have to be that way. The same lesson applies to corporate life. There is a better way to win.

START PLAYING EARLY—
WITH THE RIGHT SCORECARD

Very few people reflect on a character scorecard for their life. It's just not a concept that many consider. Society has its own not-so-subtle scorecard, as we have seen. We're used to a scorecard in golf, in baseball, in lots of athletic endeavors. We're used to report cards in school. We're used to assessments at work—employer performance evaluations, 360s, sales quotas, etc. We're used to the occasional health exam, annual checkups, and health risk assessments.

Golf is not as much fun without a scorecard. Tennis doesn't work as well without it. Same for other sports. Somehow, though, we muddle through life without a scorecard, one that's focused on character strengths, even though most people, if they reflected on it, would agree that in the game of life, these are what truly matter most.

How is it we missed that?

In the comedy *City Slickers*, the hapless hero Mitch (Billy Crystal) learns an important life lesson from the grizzled old cowboy Curly (the incomparable Jack Palance).

Curly: Do you know what the secret of life is? [pause]
  This. [holds up one finger]
Mitch: Your finger?
Curly: One thing. Just one thing. You stick to that and
  the rest don't mean shit.
Mitch: But what is the "one thing"?
Curly: [smiles] That's what you have to find out.

Let's face it: Designing a life scorecard takes some serious, soulful reflection. Even when there are no storm clouds on the horizon, forces are so intense, and so many things are going on in life, that it can be hard to focus on what really matters. How do we see the big picture when there are bills to pay, the endless demands of child-rearing, immediate health issues, long-term career advancement, job uncertainty, relationship issues, aging parents, and on and on and on? How do we engage meaningfully with such an important topic when the only solitude we know is in the ten seconds right before we drift off to sleep, at the end of another long, exhausting day, barely able to hold a lucid (much less a deep) thought in our heads? It almost seems as if our workaday existence conspires to keep us from finding that solitude we require to construct a meaningful scorecard for life.

In a 2009 lecture he delivered to the plebe class at the United States Military Academy at West Point, writer William Deresiewicz argued that solitude is one of the most important necessities of great leadership. It is the only way one can formulate solid answers to life's big questions: "Am I doing the right thing with my life? Do I believe the things I was taught as a child? What do the words I live by—words like duty, honor and country—really mean? Am I happy?" For Deresiewicz, solitude is the very essence of leadership.

There is hardly a more moving or real scene than the one in *Saving Private Ryan* in which Private Ryan, now an old man, stands amid the gravestones at the military cemetery at Normandy and says quietly, pleadingly, to his wife, "Tell me I have led a good life."

It's no wonder so many of us fail seriously to ponder life's big questions until our twilight years, when the pace of life finally slows down. Unfortunately, by then so much time has passed, so many growth opportunities have been missed, so little time is left on our biological clocks. When we find the solitude to reflect honestly on all the sacrifices people have made since we were born so that we could have our chance at life, so we could do something significant with our life, we cannot help but feel a deep sense of responsibility, as well as an urgency to "repay" this extraordinary gift.

A NEW WAY TO DREAM

"I want to be a billionaire. I want to be on the cover of *Forbes* magazine."

"I want to win the World Series MVP." "I want to win an Oscar."

"I want to cure cancer." "I want to be president."

"I want to be first in my class." "I want to be rich and famous."

Why doesn't any kid ever say, "I want to become a person of great character, depth, and wisdom"?

Society encourages our children to dream about their futures— about being an astronaut, surgeon, scientist, professional athlete, actor, musician, to discover a medical breakthrough. The implicit assumption is that if you can achieve these things, you will be successful, happy, and fulfilled. You will be someone.

What we want most for ourselves and our children, as we have learned, comes from intrinsic, not extrinsic, pursuits. Thus, if happiness, stable self-esteem, and inner peace are intrinsically driven, why don't we encourage those we influence to dream accordingly? To dream differently? We don't encourage our children to dream about such things because we were never encouraged to do so. We tend to do what our parents were conditioned by society to do. It's that simple.

Given how fabulous kids are at dreaming, given how resonant and emotionally powerfully dreams can be, how much is lost—or at least made significantly more difficult—by having kids *not* dream of things that almost assuredly *would* make them more fulfilled, things that actually *are* within their control and eminently achievable?

It's been our experience at the Institute that children as young as nine years old can be taught to dream about matters of character through tennis. We've learned that they are not only capable of dreaming in this new way, they are thoroughly excited and inspired about doing so! And what about their dreams to cure cancer; to be lawyers, surgeons, professional athletes; or to win an Oscar? We do not want those fires diminished in any way. But there is a profound qualifier, a big one that changes how and why the extrinsic dream is pursued. This qualifier changes everything. It begins with these simple words—"I want to be a person of great character, both moral and performance, who . . . became an astronaut," ". . . became a surgeon," ". . . became a professional athlete," ". . . became an Oscar winner."

The qualifier: "I want to be a person of great character." A new way to dream.

10

Winning with Your New Scorecard

There are two things to aim at in life: First to get
what you want, and after that to enjoy it. Only the wisest of
mankind has achieved the second.

—Logan Pearsall Smith

In Andre Agassi's book *Open*, I found as good an example as I've ever come across of a person who demonstrated the desire, discipline, courage, and humility—in short, the character—to take the steps that changed everything. In his own way, Andre traded in the scorecard he'd used his whole life, one that had brought incredible extrinsic reward but almost no joy—indeed, had brought great amounts of unhappiness—for a new character scorecard—one that has brought him and will continue to bring him a level of fulfillment and happiness and a sense of short- and long-term purpose that surpasses anything he had felt before.

A quick review of his journey (which I referenced in the Introduction): I first met Andre at the Nick Bollettieri Tennis Academy, when he was fourteen years old. I was responsible for the mental training of more than two hundred players there, yet Andre managed to stand out—for his rebelliousness, sarcasm, obstinacy, anger. He also stood out for his phenomenal physical ability: It was clear he had more than enough talent to play professionally someday, and possibly even to thrive in those ranks; far less clear was whether he had the mental, emotional, and psychological strength to meet the challenges he would inevitably face in that world, and in the grown-up world generally. From Andre's first memories, his father had demanded things of him that made Andre constantly on edge. Reading Andre tell of his near-constant psychological pain was not at all surprising to me; any adult of minimal insight who'd met him in those teen years would have sensed it almost immediately.

Andre *did* succeed as a pro, of course, spectacularly so, but his life was a stunning rebuke to the largely accepted notion that success breeds happiness. The achievements mattered hardly at all to him. He was unhappy, unfulfilled, at war with himself virtually all the time. As for his feelings about tennis, this thing at which he was so good and that had been the vehicle for all his extrinsic achievements—victory, wealth, fame, adulation? He hated it. He dared not say that in public, though, for fear that the admission would be misunderstood.★

In 1997, Andre's world ranking fell out of the top 100. Then, at his lowest, Andre found the courage to reinvent himself by aligning his tennis to his newly discovered purpose in life—"to make each other feel safe." Connecting his profession to his grand purpose for living turned tennis into a priceless gift. While he was still ostensibly chasing external achievements, he had established a new reason for doing so. In 1998, he pursued a new path: no drugs; a rigorous conditioning program; complete commitment to exorcising his demons. He ended 1999 as the world's number-one-ranked player. Happiness breeds success, not the other way around. In 2001, the Andre Agassi Charitable Foundation opened the Agassi College Preparatory Academy in his hometown of Las Vegas, a K–12 public charter school for at-risk children. In the years since, Andre has raised more than sixty million dollars and devotes much of his life to helping at-risk children.

★ Interestingly, this fear of admitting his hatred for tennis—that he might be regarded as spoiled or ungrateful for not appreciating the blessing of his talent—was probably based on the justified belief that *most* of us think that success breeds happiness; if we didn't, why would Andre have hesitated to admit how much he hated tennis?

His book tells the story of his amazing journey. When I consider the distance Andre traveled from the troubled, confused, self-absorbed, fragile teenager to the compassionate, generous, thoughtful, and humble person he is today, I am both awed and inspired. In the end, Andre used the powerful forces of his job, tennis, to become the person he most wanted to be. Ironically, the very game he hated so much became his transformative agent. He used the very thing that had stolen his life and sense of value to get them back. As long as Andre tried to fill his emptiness through winning, by seeking more fame, money, fan adoration, and stardom, the more lost he became. Only when he stopped following Society's Scorecard and started following his own did things turn around. He found a pathway for building his sense of personal value and security; in the process, he developed character traits and virtues that make us all proud. It's not all the wins and titles that inspire us so much as the man behind the victories.

In a speech he made to U.S. Open fans following his final match, in September of 2006, Andre said the following: "The scoreboard said I lost today, but what the scoreboard doesn't say is what it is I have found. Over the last twenty-one years I found loyalty: You have pulled for me on the court, and also in life. I have found inspiration: You have willed me to succeed, sometimes even in my lowest moments. And I have found generosity: You have given me your shoulders to stand on, to reach for my dreams—dreams I could have never reached without you. Over the last twenty-one years I have found you, and I will take you and the memory of you with me for the rest of my life."

IN THE DESPERATE HOURS

Andre was lucky. For all the internal pain he suffered for years, he found his way at a relatively young age and now gets to live that life, following that purposeful plan, for years to come.

Things aren't always so neat.

Some of the people I see don't find the right Ultimate Mission, and thus can't create a scorecard based on it, until later in life; at that point, they may not have the health and years to live the life the way they would have hoped. Then again, getting it right in these later-in-life instances is at least as crucial as it is for the younger person. It is in such trying moments, after all, where motivation is *most* needed, if we're to give our best energy for those around us, and for our legacy.

I first met John Gross about five years ago, when he came through our program. He was forty-seven at the time, an upper-level executive, married, with one young son. He lived in Orlando, not far from the Institute. We'd had a nodding acquaintanceship around the golf and tennis club that abuts the Institute; sometimes I'd see him at the club with his wife, Sue, after a round of golf. One day, John asked if he could attend my workshop—he'd been hearing positive things from others in the area—and I told him of course. He attended the next open-enrollment program. Right away I could tell he was one of those who would reap great benefit: He approached his time there with the utmost seriousness and open-mindedness.

After the workshop, we maintained our now more-than-nodding acquaintanceship, and every so often he would tell me how he had integrated the insights and rituals he had learned in the workshop into his day-to-day life—keeping gratitude logs, continually reframing his situation, converting storms into opportunities for growth—and how dramatically for the better things had changed for him.

About a year ago it dawned on me that I hadn't seen John for quite some time, but I realized it in that way you do with someone who isn't a close friend or daily colleague. The thought came to me, I noted it, it passed.

About eight months later, I received an email from John.

He wanted me to know that he had been diagnosed with amyotrophic lateral sclerosis—ALS, better known as Lou Gehrig's disease. The disease, I knew, attacks the nerve cells in the brain and spinal cord that control voluntary muscle movement. Unlike some diseases and conditions, ALS does not wax and wane, but in the vast majority of instances only ever gets worse; it is, to this point, incurable. It killed Gehrig at age thirty-seven and has killed thousands of others, many at distressingly young ages. John was fifty-two years old when I got his email.

He began to send me periodic emails documenting his condition and his response to his new circumstances. I was terribly saddened to hear about the fate that had befallen John, of course, but I was also riveted every time I received another "progress" email from him. Since I rarely saw him in person anymore, it was generally the only word I had of him.

Here's one of John's email updates:

EXECUTIVE SUMMARY

1) Speaking has become 80 percent impossible.
2) Still able to swallow.
3) Still able to walk with a walker.
4) Still breathing okay but sense material loss of muscle strength.
5) Am disappointed at rate of loss of strength in upper body.
6) I cannot raise a 2lb weight above chin level with either right or left arm.
7) I was bicep curling 15lbs now down to 5lb. Grip is so weak I have trouble holding weights
8) I manage but cannot easily move my arms to eat, touch the top of my head, brush teeth etc. The arms feel heavy all the time
9) Am mildly impressed with lower body strength having leg ext at peak of 155lb, pressed 240lb.
10) Leg curls are weak with 50lbs my peak.
11) Noticed strength across range of motion is uneven. [example: pressing 240 was easy; pressing 150lbs with knees in chest was hard.]
12) I feel rate of decline has accelerated or maybe I am crossing thresholds of functionality and realizing day to day losses.

13) Cardio seems okay but output has dropped from peak spikes of 1000 calories per hour to 750 to 350. It's harder to push heart rate above 145.

14) Weight is stable but I want to trend from 35% body fat to 20 slowly. I am on the way.

So much for the technical, physical aspects of his life. John continued:

I am mostly cherishing moments even as I decline figuring I can't leave any moment wasted. Without emotion pills for 5 days there is no difference. Faith is strong. I have started sending memories to my wife Sue and son Hunter daily. Still do gratitude logs daily. Still have not felt sorry for myself yet and I wonder if I will sustain that fact. I REFRAME DAILY ON MY DECLINE AND COMPETE AGAINST THE NEW CAPABILITY.

John was not done with his update.

WSJ article regarding Sign on a hospital door of injured Navy SEAL Fall 2009

"Don't feel sorry for me. The wounds I received I got in a job I love, doing it for people I love, supporting the freedom of a country I deeply love. I am incredibly tough. I promise a full recovery. This hospital room is a place of fun, optimism, and intense and rapid re-growth. If you are not prepared for that, GO ELSEWHERE."

"The Management"

My version:

Don't feel sorry for me. The fate I received I got during a job I love, doing it for a family I love, supporting the Christian values I deeply love, having enjoyed life experiences better than 99% of the history of mankind. I aspire to match the example of those that are incredibly tough. I promise my son and my wife that their recovery will be full whatever my outcome. My life is a place of fun, optimism, and intense and rapid growth even now! If you are not prepared for that then GO ELSEWHERE.

Jim—
YOUR PROGRAM HAS GIVEN ME THE RITUALS AND PERSPECTIVE TO FIND COURAGE. SPECIFICALLY BECAUSE I HAD AN ULTIMATE MISSION IN PLACE I WAS ABLE TO CONVERT THE STORM INTO RAIN THAT RENEWS LIFE RATHER THAN A STORM THAT TAKES LIFE. [YOU COULD WELL CALL THIS THE ULTIMATE TEST FOR THE ULTIMATE MISSION]

Sad as John's tale is, I find (and hope you will, too) that it validates all the more the urgent need to examine one's scorecard and Ultimate Mission and revise them—whether with minor tweaks or a massive overhaul—so that one can move forward, for the long haul. In one's most desperate hours—as John has surely found himself—it is this security, along with his faith, that help him make the most out of his otherwise difficult days. Today's world has more than its share of people in the latter part of their lives growing increasingly bitter about their possibilities (to be fair, every era surely has this). John dealt with his decline by "refram[ing it] daily" and "compet[ing] against the new capability." He sets a remarkable example for Sue, Hunter (now thirteen), and for all of us. John passed away November 1, 2011.

Gene O'Kelly, the hard-driving CEO and chairman of KPMG who in the book *Chasing Daylight* chronicled the countdown to his death, at age fifty-three, of an inoperable brain tumor, was, like my friend John Gross, someone who had braced himself in his final chapter: Gene eventually found a sense of purpose and inner peace that had often eluded him when he was younger and climbing the corporate ladder. He found that by investing his diminishing energy in those people and issues that mattered most to him, a deep sense of fulfillment and gratitude emerged. And if you're thinking that anyone with a death sentence would naturally do this, it turns out, sadly, that that's not the case. Gene's odyssey did not surprise me: I was fortunate enough to work with him about a year before he fell ill, and I could sense then that he was on a mission to define a grander sense of purpose. Indeed, he was beginning to find it—not just for himself, but for the many people who worked under him at KPMG, where he began to implement a program for the entire leadership that began with each person defining his or her version of the Ultimate Mission. When Gene was diagnosed with brain cancer soon after, he was in a far better position to handle the awful news than if he had been focused, as so many corporate executives are, on mere extrinsic success and milestones.

Of course, if you have your scorecard perfectly right from the beginning—though such a scenario is quite rare—then you are equipped for when even the most terrible storms darken the skies. When Jill Costello, a coxswain for the University of California-Berkeley crew team, finished her junior year, she discovered that she had stage IV lung cancer, a particularly shocking diagnosis for an otherwise healthy, athletic, twenty-one-year-old nonsmoker. In the November 29, 2010, issue of *Sports Illustrated*, writer Chris Ballard tells the story of the last year in the life of this remarkable young woman, who wrote,

> *Your life is happening right now and this is the only moment you can control. This is the only minute that really matters. If you are constantly dwelling on something that happened in the past or feeling anxious about the future, you are missing out on YOUR LIFE. Do what makes you happy in this moment and your life will be full.*

These are the words of someone who will not allow herself to be controlled by extrinsic factors, not even stage IV lung cancer, chemo, nausea, etc. This is someone who is engaged fully in life and in that which she can control, just as she had been for all the years leading up to her terrible illness; someone genuinely mindful of the moment; someone not waiting for something to happen before she can experience joy but, instead, finding joy in the joyful activities that are already in her life. It can come as no surprise that Jill Costello had always possessed an immense array of character strengths, particularly moral: She loved people and cared about them deeply her entire short life. She was someone who made those around her happier and better. In college she volunteered at Habitat for Humanity, even as she was active in a sorority, was deeply involved in campus life, and carried a full academic and athletic load. She was known as the first person to make a new kid in school feel welcome; known for her humor; known for her thoughtfulness (when her roommate took a semester away, Jill texted her every day to say good morning and good night); known for her sense of responsibility and caring (she got her Class B driver's license so she could drive the team van, then rose at 5:30 A.M. six days a week to pick up the rowers for practice). She had a cornucopia of performance character strengths and moral character strengths. She had character through and through. She had the right scorecard.

JESSICA'S SCORECARD AND POSITIVE LIFE

The first part of Jessica's story was discussed in Chapter 6. To refresh your memory, Jessica was a forty-three-year-old executive married with two children. Despite all her success—an MBA from Dartmouth, salary in excess of $300,000, etc.—she was frustrated and unfulfilled with her life. She was driven, hard on herself and others, and fragile—a perfectionist. Her relentless inner voice and her race to achieve blocked her over and again. Now for the rest of her story . . .

Jessica's life took a new, positive direction. The breakthrough began when, after several hours of deep reflection while doing her homework on the evening of Day 1 of the program, she was able to determine her Ultimate Mission in life. Writing about her "best self" and crystallizing who she really wanted to be released a torrent of emotion. In her own words, "I cried and cried and cried. I wasn't clear why all the tears were flowing but clearly a nerve was touched that went deep into my soul. It was an amazing moment for me. I don't think I'll ever forget it. What I felt was a strange mix of pain and remorse, hope, and inspiration." It was the first time Jessica had truly ever faced the truth about who she had become and who she desperately wanted to be as a mother, wife, and friend. And Jessica did not run from the storm she created within herself. She began to write and write until she could describe with great clarity who she was now and how she felt about it. At HPI, we call this her "old story." In the evening of Day 2, Jessica wrote her new story, and with it came a powerful commitment to change, one that had little to do with herself and everything to do with those she loved and cared most about. Here's just a part of what she wrote:

> My relentless quest for perfection and my critical attitude toward myself and others were simply my attempts to fill the emptiness and inadequacy I've felt inside. I now can see the futility of it all. The path I took directly undermined the things I most wanted to be—kind, loving, patient, compassionate, and grateful. Growing these attributes, I now understand, is the only way I will find the peace and fulfillment I long for. I can never get to where I want to be by chasing more worldly achievements. It hasn't worked for me and I know it never will.

Jessica returned to the Institute in 2011 with twelve of her direct reports. "I wanted what happened to me to happen to the people I am leading, she told her HPI account manager before returning for the second time. According to Jessica, her character scorecard and daily training log made the difference. And her 360 report confirmed that, in fact, she was becoming more of the best-self person she wanted to be. Her growth in character strengths provided the answer she was looking for.

THE LAST TIME

The scorecard is not just for people in desperate times, of course—though perhaps we ought to stop here to define "desperate times." Might one not define it as "an unsatisfactory, even despairing time that demands to be changed, urgently"? John, Gene, Jill, and Jessica's stories demonstrate vividly that there truly is no time to put off the task of formulating your Ultimate Mission and writing out the scorecard that works for you. Without it, navigating the treacherous seas of life—the seductions, the fake treasures, the inevitable losses—all too often exceeds our capacity.

With it, armed with purpose and meaning, a remarkable inner strength and grit emerges, paving the way for sustaining happiness and fulfillment, even in the worst of times.

John Gross, Gene O'Kelly, Jill Costello—did not get to pick their plight. To an extent, none of us do. We *can*, however, pick how we live our lives, how fulfilling they can be, and the legacy we leave for those we love.

And though it happens sooner or more abruptly for some than for others, for each and every activity in which we engage there is surely a "last time." There will be a last time that I get to play tennis, which has been a supreme gift in my life. If I walk out on the court and have the frame of reference that this could be the last time, I am so much more engaged and connected in the time and energy I am investing. If it's windy or cold, if I'm not playing well, if there are things that would ordinarily frustrate me—they all disappear in the face of this time being, possibly, The Last Time.

There will be a last time I will be able to sprint in my workouts, which I love to do.

There will be a last time when I take an adventure vacation with my three sons.

There will be a last time that I will share a Christmas or Thanksgiving with my mother, who is ninety-six years old.

We rarely know when the last time will happen; it is recognizable to us only in retrospect, if at all. But simply reflecting on The Last Time changes everything. It drives urgency to the present. It makes everything in the now more precious.

For everything, there is a last time—a last time to formulate your Ultimate Mission, a last time to grow your character and the character of those you care most about. Create your Ultimate Mission and your scorecard and do it now, not at some undefined time in the future.

And let your scorecard be truly yours—purposeful, enriching, and grounded in ethical/moral character; a scorecard truly worth dying for, and living for.

START NOW

Get a pencil. Write down, after soulful deliberation, what you believe to be your Ultimate Mission in life:

_____

_____

_____

_____

_____

_____

Now write down the ethical/moral character strengths that are must-haves if you are to complete that Ultimate Mission.

1. _____

2. _____

3. _____

4. _____

5. _____

You are back to chasing achievement again—only this time you're armed with a new scorecard that re-purposes all achievements as opportunities for developing strengths of character. As you've learned from these pages, the only enduring path to achievement fulfillment at work and in life is making sure character trumps all other considerations. It is, truly, the only way to win.

ACKNOWLEDGMENTS

First to my parents, Mary and Con, for brilliantly modeling strong character in every aspect of their lives.

To my three sons, Mike, Pat, and Jeff, who continue to be my greatest source of joy and inspiration.

To Jack Groppel, my business partner from the beginning, for your always loyal support and cherished friendship.

To Andy Postman, for his extraordinary writing skills and help with this project. Andy, your encouragement, passion for the topic, competence, and professionalism make you a great joy to work with.

To Becky Hoholski, for your tireless commitment to this manuscript from Day One. Your capacity and attention to detail is beyond remarkable. You never failed to bring order and harmony to the chaos. Thank you for your commitment over so many years.

To Matt Inman, for his brilliant editing and crafting of the manuscript.

To Richard Pine and all of Inkwell, for believing in this book and charting a path to publishing success.

To Chris Osorio, for your enduring friendship, leadership, and countless contributions to my life.

To all the HPI staff, of whom I am so proud—especially Bill Donovan, Raquel Malo Garzon, Steve Page, Chris Jordan, Lorenzo Beltrame, Mike Florence, Caroline Rivera.

To Bill Weldon, for believing we could make a real difference in the world.

To Calvin Schmidt, for your support of this project, for your leadership, and for affording me the time to invest in this effort.

To all the athletes who have touched my life and formed the basis of my thinking, and to the countless thought leaders and researchers who have inspired this work.

To my brother Tom and my sister Jane (Sister Mary Margaret Loehr), whose depth of character, compassion for others, and courage are constant sources of inspiration to me.

To Tom Gullikson, Steve Reinemund, George Dom, Ray Smith, Fred Harburg, John Ratey, Sanjay Gupta, Vic Strecher, Ben Wiegand, Kevin Wildenhaus, Michelle Goodrich, Scott Cassidy, Kevin Accola, Michael Johnson, Cat and Jessica Bradu, Jim Courier, Dan Jansen, Tom Davin, Randy Gerber, Will Marre, Paul Hancock, Tim Heckler, Charlie Kim, Paul Roetert, Peter Scaturro, Bill and Mary Rompf, Renate Gaisser, Kevin Kempin, Greg Mason, Amy Wishingrad, Dennis and Pat Van der Meer, Dan Santorum, and Peter Borer.

Finally, to Vickie and Bob Zoellner and to Gordon Uehling, for giving me the chance to pursue my dream.

FURTHER READING

Agassi, Andre. *Open.*

Anchor, Shawn. *The Happiness Advantage.*

Ben-Shara, Tal. *The Pursuit of Perfect.*

Brim, Orville Gilbert. *Look at Me.*

Brooks, David. *The Social Animal.*

Brown, Bruce. *Teaching Character Through Sport.*

Buettner, Dan. *Thrive.*

Callahan, David. *The Cheating Culture.*

Chopra, Deepak. *The Seven Spiritual Laws of Superheroes.*

Chua, Amy. *Battle Hymn of the Tiger Mother.*

Clifford, Craig, and Randolph Feezel. *Sport and Character.*

Coyle, Daniel. *The Talent Code.*

Diener, Ed, and Robert Biswas-Diener. *Happiness.*

Dohrmann, George. *Play Their Hearts Out.*

Dungy, Tony, David Robinson, Tom Osborne, et al. *The Greatest Coach Ever: Timeless Wisdom and Insights of John Wooden.*

Dweck, Carol S. *Mindset.*

Dweck, Carol S. *Self-Theories.*

Dweck, Carol S., and Jutta Heckhausen. *Motivation and Self-Regulation Across the Life Span.*

Farrey, Tom. *Game On.*

Frederickson, Barbara. *Positivity.*

Ginsburg, Richard, Stephen Durant, and Amy Baltzell. *Whose Game Is It, Anyway?*

Gongwer, Todd. *Lead . . . for God's Sake.*

Goodwin, Doris Kearns. *Lyndon Johnson and the American Dream.*

Graden, John. *The Imposter Syndrome.*

Handy, Charles. *The Age of Paradox.*

Hagger, Martin, and Nikos Chatzisarantis. *Intrinsic Motivation and Self-Determination in Exercise and Sport.*

Hallowell, Ed. *The Childhood Roots of Adult Happiness.*

Halpern, Jake. *Fame Junkies.*

Hyman, Mark. *Until It Hurts.*

Isaacs, David. *Character Building.*

Karayeorghis, Costas, and Pete Terry. *Inside Sport Psychology.*

Kasser, Tim. *The High Price of Materialism.*

Kessler, Ron. *In the President's Secret Service.*

Kindlon, Dan. *Too Much of a Good Thing.*

Krakauer, Jon. *Into Thin Air.*

Kushner, Harold. *When All You've Every Wanted Isn't Enough.*

Lawrence, Cooper. *The Cult of Perfection.*

Levine, Madeline. *The Price of Privilege.*

Lickona, Thomas. *Character Matters.*

Lowe, Rob. *Stories I Only Tell My Friends.*

Lyubomirsky, Sonja. *The How of Happiness.*

McBride, Karyl. *Will I Ever Be Good Enough?*

McClelland, David C. *The Achievement Motive.*

McClelland, David C. *The Achieving Society.*

Morgan, William. *Ethics in Sport.*

Myers, David G. *The American Paradox.*

O'Kelly, Eugene. *Chasing Daylight.*

O'Neill, Jessie. *The Golden Ghetto.*

Peterson, Christopher, and Martin Seligman. *Character Strengths and Virtues.*

Pink, Daniel H. *Drive.*

Robbins, Alexandra. *The Overachievers.*

Rubens, Jim. *OverSuccess.*

Seligman, Martin E. P. *Authentic Happiness.*

Seligman, Martin E. P. *Flourish.*

Seligman, Martin E. P. *Learned Optimism.*

Stanley, Thomas J. *The Millionaire Mind.*

Twenge, Jean. *Generation Me.*

Twenge, Jean, and Keith Campbell. *The Narcissism Epidemic.*

Vallerand, Robert J., and Catherine F. Ratelle (edited by E. Deci and R. Ryan). *The Handbook of Self-Determination.*

Waddington, Ivan, and Andy Smith. *Drugs in Sport.*

Williams, Pat. *Coach Wooden: The 7 Principles That Shaped His Life and Will Change Yours.*

Williams, Pat. *How to Be Like Coach Wooden: Life Lessons from Basketball's Greatest Leader.*

Yorkey, Mike. *Playing with Purpose.*

Young-Eisendrath, Polly. *The Self-Esteem Trap.*

Notes

INTRODUCTION

4   as well-being experts Ed Diener and Robert Biswas-Diener . . . "but the exchange rate isn't great": Ed Diener and Robert Biswas-Diener, *Happiness: Unlocking the Mysteries of Psychological Wealth* (New York: Blackwell, 2008), 111.

5   "What the hell is wrong with me? . . . wrong goals": Andre Agassi, *Open: An Autobiography* (New York: Knopf, 2009), 204.

5   "I've been let in on a dirty little secret: winning changes nothing.": Ibid., 167.

6   "I try to talk myself out . . . own your own plane.": Ibid., 231.

7   "This is the only perfection there is . . . make each other feel safe.": Ibid., 231.

CHAPTER 1. A PARADE OF FAILED PROMISES

13   "We are never deceived; we deceive ourselves."—Goethe: quotationspage.com/quote/1743.html (from *The Sorrows of Young Werther*).

15–16 "We are born with the powerful urge . . . our environment," write A. J. Elliot, H. A. McGregor, and T. M. Thrash: "The Need for Competence," *Handbook of Self-Determination Research* (Rochester, NY: University of Rochester Press. 2002), 361.

16–17 "So much of our society . . . sufficient reason to be there.": climb.mountainzone.com/interviews/2001/weathers/ html/.

18 "It's not the mountain we conquer, but ourselves": en.wikiquote.org/wiki/Edmund_Hillary.

18 An alarming 40 percent . . . clinically obese: prnewswire.com/ news-releases/new-study-finds-4-of-10-top-executives-are -obese-72590562.html.

21 In his excellent book *The High Price of Materialism* . . . "worth $13 billion": Tim Kasser, *The High Price of Materialism* (Cambridge, MA: MIT Press, 2002), 43.

23 "If work is inherently enjoyable . . . become less necessary.": Daniel Pink, *Drive* (New York: Penguin, 2009), 31.

27 Research has shown that "rewarding employees . . . more unethical behavior than they would otherwise.": Max H. Bazerman and Ann E. Tenbrunsel, "Ethical Breakdowns," *Harvard Business Review*, April 2011, 61–62.

28 That's how it happened to Scott Sullivan . . . allegations of massive fraud.: David Callahan, *The Cheating Culture* (New York: Harcourt, 2004), 106.

28 There's a willingness, as David Callahan . . . "money and career.": Ibid., 106.

CHAPTER 2. HOW DID WE GET HERE?

31 "They were so strong in their beliefs . . . what exactly those beliefs were."—Louise Erdrich: quotationspage.com/ quote/1624.html.

32 In his book *Character Matters*, Thomas Lickona writes, "The family . . . about love": Thomas Lickona, *Character Matters* (New York: Touchstone, 2004), xxiv.

32–33 In his book *The Millionaire Mind*, Thomas J. Stanley . . . Integrity: Thomas J. Stanley, *The Millionaire Mind* (Kansas City, MO: Andrews McMeel, 2001), 52.

33 "The proper time to influence . . . hundred years before he's

born.": William R. Inge: josephsoninstitute.org/quotes/quota
tions.php?q=Parenting.

33–34 "According to Bronnie Ware . . . not the life others expected of me.' ": hospicepatients.org/five-regrets-of-the-dying
-bronnie-ware.html.

35 The reasons may also be divided . . . activity for its own sake:
Elliot and Harakiewicz, *Journal of Personality and Social Psychology* 70, no. 3 (1996): 462.

35 Extrinsic motivation refers to behavior . . . avoid an external
punishment.: M. Vansteenkiste, B. Suenens, and W. Lens,
"Intrinsic Versus Extrinsic Goal Promotion in Exercise and
Sport," in M. Hagger and N. Chatzisarantis, *Intrinsic Motivation
and Self-Determination in Exercise and Sport* (Champaign, IL:
Human Kinetics, 2007).

35 "I do not know the key to success . . . Make everybody happy":
en.wikiquote.org/wiki/Success.

36 The latest research shows that high self-esteem . . . violence,
smoking, drinking, or taking drugs: R. F. Baumeister, J. D.
Campbell, J. L. Krueger, and K. D. Vohs, "Does high self-
esteem cause better performance, interpersonal success, happiness or healthier lifestyles?" *Psychological Science in the Public
Interest* 4 (2003): 1–44.

36 One of the only positives is the connection . . . feelings of
happiness.: E. Diener and M. Diener, "Cross-cultural Correlates of Life Satisfaction and Self-Esteem," *Journal of Personality
and Social Psychology* 69 (1995): 120–29.

36–37 Students who based their self-esteem . . . not lack of ability:
J. Crocker, A. T. Brook, Y. Niiya, M. Villacorta, "The Pursuit
of Self-Esteem: Contingencies of Self-Worth and Self-
Regulation," *Journal of Personality* 74, no. 6 (December 2006):
1762.

37 "What kind of man makes it through Hell Week . . . you
do—or you do not": wsj.com/article/SB1000142405274870399
27045763070213392104888.html.

37 Janelle Cambron and Linda Acitelli reported in . . . "quality of their friendships": M. Janelle Cambron and Linda K. Acitelli, "Examining the Link Between Friendship Contingent Self-Esteem and the Self-Propagating Cycle of Depression," *Journal of Social and Clinical Psychology* 29, no. 6 (2010).

38 Self-Esteem Is Not a Basic Need: R. Ryan and K. W. Brown, "Why We Don't Need Self-Esteem: On Fundamental Needs, Contingent Love and Mindfulness," *Psychological Inquiry* 14, no. 1 (2003): 73.

39 The writer Fran Lebowitz . . . "to have self-esteem.": time.com/time/arts/article/0,8599,2032523,00.html

40 According to Jean Twenge . . . "self-esteem is an outcome, not a cause": Jean Twenge, *Generation Me* (New York: Free Press, 2006), 66.

40 Dr. Roy Baumeister, professor of psychology . . . "concentrate more on self-control and self-discipline.": Ibid.

41 In a study conducted by the University of Rochester . . . depressed mood and health problems.: physorg.com/news161516559.html; kellymcgonigal.blogspot.com/2009/06/study-wealth-fame-and-beauty-make-your.html.

41 Carol Dweck has done . . . determining outlook: Carol S. Dweck, *Mindset* (New York: Random House, 2006).

41 Jennifer Crocker and Lora Park argue . . . "would seem to have fewer costs": "The Costly Pursuit of Self-Esteem," *Psychological Bulletin* 130, no. 3 (2004): 404.

43 According to theorists Edward . . . internally imposed demands: *Handbook of Self-Determination Research* (New York: University of Rochester Press, 2002), 354.

44 "The mechanism of most addictive drugs . . . nucleus accumbens": Daniel Pink, *Drive* (New York: Riverhead, 2009), 55.

44–45 "Our neurons quickly adapt . . . cashmere sweater": Jonah Lehrer, "Shopping, Depression and Dopamine," scienceblogs.com/cortex/2006/12/post_8.php, December 11, 2006.

45 famously dubbed this phenomenon . . . "the hedonic tread-
    mill": Brickman, Philip, and Donald Campbell, "Hedonic
    Relativism and Planning the Good Society," in M. Appley,
    Adaptation-level Theory: A Symposium (NewYork: Academic
    Press, 1971), 287–302, http://en.wikipedia.org/wiki/Hedonic
    _treadmill.

45 "Truth be told . . . 'Is that all there is?')": Rob Lowe, *Stories I
    Only Tell My Friends*, (New York: Holt, 2011), 115.

45 "We are wired to always . . . much we already have": Jonah
    Lehrer, "Shopping, Depression and Dopamine," scienceblogs
    .com/cortex/2006/12/post_8.php, December 11, 2006.

46 There is evidence that vulnerability . . . nucleus accumbens.:
    J. W. Dalley, et al., "Nucleus Accumbens D2/3 Receptors
    Predict Trait Impulsivity and Cocaine Reinforcement," *Science*
    315, 5816, (March 2, 2007): 1267–70.

46 To quote Christopher Lasch, "Drugs are merely . . . our soci-
    ety.": famousquotes.com/author/christopher-lasch/ (from *The
    True and Only Heaven: Progress and Its Critics*)

CHAPTER 3. THE CRY FOR A NEW SCORECARD

50 At least one study found . . . that lasts roughly two years: Sonja
    Lyubomirsky, *The How of Happiness* (New York: Penguin,
    2007), 49.

50–51 Another study points out . . . brought more problems than it
    solved: Ibid., 44.

51 A 2008 study . . . spending on others and charity did, signifi-
    cantly so: livescience.com/health/080320-happiness-money
    .html.

51 An astonishing 94 percent . . . relief after fifteen days: Sonja
    Lyubomirsky, *The How of Happiness* (New York: Penguin,
    2007), 15.

52 successful marriage: Spend five . . . has done for you: Ibid.,
    142.

52 "Making other people . . . true happiness": Ibid., 125.

52 Compassion for others may have . . . "you're going to struggle": Kirsten Weir, "Golden Rule Redux," *Monitor on Psychology* 42, no.7 (July/August 2011): 42–45.

52 "Our souls are hungry . . . live so that our lives matter": Harold Kushner, *When All You've Ever Wanted Isn't Enough* (New York: Fireside, 1986). 18.

53 "At last my fame will have a purpose": Andre Agassi, *Open* (New York: Knopf, 2009), 261.

55 "Many persons have a wrong idea . . . through fidelity to a worthy purpose": Helen Keller, "The Simplest Way to Be Happy," *Home* magazine, February 1933.

59 "Whatever the obstacles . . . 'he's part of everything we do'": Richard Eaton, "The New Normal," *TennisLife*, 15–16.

64 "In *The Handbook of Self-Determination*, Robert J. Valleran . . . of interest and enjoyment": R. Vallerand and C. Ratelle, "Intrinsic and Extrinsic Motivation: A Hierarchical Model," in Edward Deci and Richard Ryan, *The Handbook of Self-Determination* (Rochester, NY: University of Rochester Press, 2002), 42.

64 As Deci says in Daniel Pink's book, *Drive* . . . "rewards would have a negative effect": Daniel Pink, *Drive* (New York: Riverhead, 2009), 9.

66 "Goals that people set for themselves . . . dangerous side effects": Ibid., 50.

66 "None of us can . . . no human being": Harold Kushner, *When All You've Ever Wanted Isn't Enough* (New York: Fireside, 1986), 53.

68 "True fulfillment is, I believe, vicarious . . . happiness of others": Charles Handy, in *Masters of the Wired World*, edited by Anne Leer (FT.com, 1999).

68 "If you want others to be happy . . . practice compassion.": quotationspage.com/quote/31686.html.

CHAPTER 4. CHARACTER COMES IN TWO TYPES

71 "You can easily judge the character of a man . . . nothing for
him."—Goethe: http://josephsoninstitute.org/quotes/quota
tions.php?q=Character.

75 As Lickona and Davidson conclude . . . "virtues can be used for
bad ends": Thomas Lickona and Matthew Davidson, *Smart and
Good High Schools* (Center for the 4th and 5th Rs at the State
University of New York College at Cortland and the Institute
for Excellence and Ethics, 2005), 20.

80 As David Brooks writes in *The Social Animal* . . . "clash with
the competitive virtues": David Brooks, *The Social Animal*
(New York: Random House, 2011), 287.

CHAPTER 5. BUILDING YOUR SCORECARD AND TRAINING THE MUSCLES OF CHARACTER

81 "As a single footstep will not make a path on the earth . . .
wish to dominate our lives."—Henry David Thoreau: thinkex
ist.com/quotation/as_a_single_footstep_will_not_make_a
_path_on_the/344172.html.

82 The noted psychologist Leon . . . cognitive dissonance: Leon
Festinger, *Theory of Cognitive Dissonance* (Stanford University
Press, 1957).

83 Similarly, researcher Jennifer Crocker from the University of
Michigan contends . . . "other-directed feelings": J. Crocker,
Y. Niiya, and D. Mischkowski, "Why Does Writing About
Important Values Reduce Defensiveness: Self-affirmation and
the Roles of Positive Other-directed Feelings," *Psychological
Science* 19 (2008): 740.

99 "Character development. . . . spectator sport": Thomas Lickona, *Character Matters* (New York: Touchstone, 2004), 55.

100 "The moment of victory . . . nothing else": Martina Navratilova, http://www.quotationspage.com/quote/25911.html.

101 "Compared to what we ought to be, we are only half awake":
William James: great-quotes.com/quote/882388.

102 In his book *The Talent Code*, Daniel Coyle . . . "turns them into skills": Daniel Coyle, *The Talent Code* (New York: Bantam, 2009), 19–20.

102 In his book *Flourish*, Martin Seligman . . . enhance them further: Martin E. P. Seligman, *Flourish* (New York: Free Press, 2011).

104 "steely resolve . . . No shortcuts": Andre Agassi, *Open* (New York: Knopf, 2009), 271.

107 The psychologist Lawrence Kohlberg . . . of moral dilemmas: "Moral Development and Moral Education: An Overview," http://tigger.uic.edu/~lnucci/MoralEd/overview.html.

107 Researchers Paul Ekman and Harriet Oster . . . triggered changes in the physical body that corresponded to those acted-out emotions: P. Ekman and H. Oster, *The Facial Action Coding System*, (Palo Alto, CA: Consulting Psychologists Press, 1978).

108 As Daniel Coyle writes in *The Talent Code*, "Nothing you can do . . . honing the circuit": Daniel Coyle, *The Talent Code* (New York: Bantam, 2009), 87.

109 As mentioned earlier, the key to happiness has little to do with external circumstances (10 percent or less): Sonja Lyubomirsky, *The How of Happiness* (New York: Penguin, 2007), 39.

110 Human beings function optimally in the presence of positive emotions: Barbara Fredrickson, *Positivity* (New York: Crown, 2009), 21–24.

110 Carol Dweck and Martin Seligman . . . sense of well-being: Carol S. Dweck, *Mindset* (New York: Random House, 2006) and Martin E. P. Seligman, *Flourish* (New York: Free Press, 2011).

CHAPTER 6. IT'S NEVER JUST A JOB

115 "intrinsically oriented employees . . . family life": Maarten Vansteenkiste, Bart Neyrinck, et al., "On the relations among work value orientations, psychological need satisfaction and job outcomes: A self-determination theory approach," *Journal of*

Occupational and Organizational Psychology 80 (Leicester, UK: The British Psychological Society, 2007), 251–277.

115–116 "He owned a spacious ranch . . . money and travel and nice things don't matter": Doris Kearns Goodwin, *Lyndon Johnson and the American Dream* (New York: St. Martin's Press, 1991), xiii.

116 "Visitors were sometimes . . . purpose or motive for deception": Ibid., ix.

116 "could not bear to be . . . in the bathroom": Ibid., viii.

116 "had spent so many . . . death": Ibid., xvii.

116 Then he said to her: "I'd . . . their children.' ": Ibid., i.

117 "You just shake your head . . . true character of its leaders": Ronald Kessler, *In the President's Secret Service* (New York: Three Rivers Press, 2010), 36–39.

122–123 A landmark 2007 study on "work value orientations . . . a satisfying family life": Maarten Vansteenkiste, Bart Neyrinck, et al., "On the relations among work value orientations, psychological need satisfaction and job outcomes: A self-determination theory approach," *Journal of Occupational and Organizational Psychology* 80 (Leicester, UK: The British Psychological Society 2007): 251–277.

124 In a 2010 list of "blissful places to work" . . . "the opportunities to develop skills": Brian Anthony Hernandez, "US military beats out Disney as happy place to work," *Business News Daily*, October 22, 2010.

127 "As officers and employees of Enron Corp . . . honest manner": soxfirst.com/50226711/enrons_code_of_ethics.php.

128 The promise made above . . . $74 billion: en.wikipedia.org/wiki/Enron_scandal.

129 "As a partner in the communities . . . we will do it": ethics-governance.com/article/enronstatement-of-human-rights-principles.html.

129 "Our objective . . . around the world": "Lessons from World-Com," presentation by John J. Sarno, Employers Association of

New Jersey, http://www.slideshare.net/JohnJS/lessons-from
-world-com-presentation.

129 As Russ McGuire, online director of *Business Reform*
magazine . . . "greed, and results at all costs": Russ McGuire,
"WorldCom's deadly culture," *WorldNetDaily*, June 17, 2003.

130–131 Here are the mission statements of some real companies:
Research Report: *Mission Statement Impact Assessment*, August 15,
2006, published by Mission Expert and Kinetic Wisdom, Inc.

132 When formulating a code of business . . . employees are, in
fact, following the rules: www.shakethatbrain.com, "Writing a
Code of Ethics for Your Business."

133 a case study of the episode has become a Harvard Business
School staple for exemplary crisismanagement: businessweek
.com/magazine/content/11_15/b4223064555570_page_4.htm.

CHAPTER 7. WHAT BUSINESS LEADERS CAN LEARN FROM SPORT

135 "It is not by muscle, speed . . . character, and judgment."—
Cicero: thinkexist.com/quotation/it_is_not_by_muscle-speed
or_physical_dexterity /176547.html.

136 The survey, called "The Goldman Dilemma," presents . . . say
"Yes!": Bob Goldman, Patricia Bush, Ronald Klatz, "Death in
the Locker Room: Steroids and Sports," *Journal of the American
Medical Association* 252, no. 19 (1984): 2771.

136 Dr. Bob Goldman, who conducted . . . "huge in the
coffin": "Easily obtained steroids focus of debate," SI.com,
November 26, 2003, sportsillustrated.cnn.com/2003/
more/11/26/us.doping.ap.

137–138 For example, a longitudinal study conducted . . . "moral
valuing, and moral action.": S. K. Stoll and J. M. Beller, *Male/
Female Student Athlete's Moral Reasoning* (Center of Ethics,
University of Idaho), www.educ.uidaho.edu/center/measure
ments/HBVCI/findings.htm.

139–140 In an article in the . . . "contingent on doing well in that sport": Donahue, Rip, and Vallerand, "When Winning Is Everything: On Passion, Identity and Aggression in Sport," *Journal of Psychology of Sport and Exercise* 10 (2009) 526–34.

140 As they embarked on . . . engaged in competition: David Shields and Brenda Bredemeier, "Moral Reasoning in the Context of Sport," http://tigger.uic.edu/~lnucci/MoralEd/articles/shieldssport.html.

142 Also, studies have shown that competitors in team . . . engaged in individual sports: Joseph Doty, "Sports Build Character?," *Journal of College & Character* 7, no. 3 (2006): 1–9.

145 "We coaches have great influence . . . causing us to sway from the moral principles": John Wooden, *They Call Me Coach* (New York: McGraw-Hill, 2003), 99.

146 According to Wooden's own players, he never mentioned the word "winning" . . . after games: John Wooden, *Wooden: A Lifetime of Reflections on and off the Court* (New York McGraw-Hill, 1997), 88.

149 Ginsburg, Durant, and Baltzell argue that "organized sports . . . lessons about themselves and the world": R. Ginsberg, S. Durant, and A. Baltzell, *Whose Game Is It, Anyway?* (New York: Houghton Mifflin Company, 2006), 1.

149 Jack Nicklaus recounts a story . . . ever played golf: Walter Bingham, "Hold That, Tiger," *Sports Illustrated*, January 19, 1998, http://sportsillustrated.cnn.com/vault/article/magazine/MAG1142810/index.htm.

CHAPTER 8. GROWING MORAL CHARACTER IN OTHERS: FOR BUSINESS LEADERS, PARENTS, TEACHERS, AND COACHES

155 "Nothing can bring you peace but the triumph of principles": Ralph Waldo Emerson, "Self-Reliance."

163 The three things parents most want for their kids . . . healthy, stable self-esteem: Edward M. Hallowell, M.D., *The Childhood Roots of Adult Happiness* (New York: Ballantine, 2002), 1–2.

163 Approximately one in fifty NCAA senior football players will
get drafted by a National Football League (NFL) team: ncaa.
org/wps/portal/ncaahome?WCM_GLOBAL_CONTEXT=/
ncaa/NCAA/Academics+and+Athletes/Education+and+
Research/Probability+of+Competing/Methodology+-+Prob
+of+Competing.

163 The average career span is approximately 3.6 years: war-
sawsportsreview.com/2011/02/josh-luchs-joins-university
-compliance-officers-at-uo-law-conference/.

163 "according to a 2006 report in the *St. Petersburg Times*, for
every season a player spends on an NFL roster, his life expectancy decreases by almost three years.": G. Doyel, "NFL is
killing its players, and the league doesn't care," CBSSports.
com, December 23, 2010, cbssports.com/print/nfl/story/
14477196/nfl-is-killing-its-players-and-league-doesnt-care.

166 Of those included in *Who's Who* . . . 80 percent agreed that
"it's not worth it to lie or cheat because it hurts your character": Thomas Lickona, *Why Character Matters* (New York:
Touchstone, 2004), 13–14.

166 In a more recent survey . . . using the Internet to plagiarize.:
charactercounts.org/programs/reportcard/2010/installment02
_report-card_honesty-integrity.html.

166 A 2009 study in *Ethics & Behavior* . . . some form of cheating:
Amy Novotney, "Beat the Cheat," *Monitor on Psychology* (June
2011): 54.

166–167 According to the 2010 CIRP Freshman Survey . . . those
two categories: newsroom.ucla.edu/portal/ucla/incoming-
college-students-self-191135.aspx.

168 If the parents who advocate the above . . . suffocating combination: Amy Chua, *Battle Hymn of the Tiger Mother* (New York:
Penguin Press HC, 2011).

169 As author Michael Lewis has written, "In Japan . . . highly
shamed situation": http://www.1-famous-quotes.com/quote/
1438100.

171 "This overly forgiving style probably came up . . . that's not good, either": Carol Milstone, "When Bad Kids Think They're Great," *National Post* (Canada), March 23, 1999.

171 As Carol Dweck writes, "One can hardly walk . . . how smart they are": Carol S. Dweck, *Self-Theories* (London: Psychology Press, 2000), 1–2.

172 Dr. Baumeister decries "giving everyone a trophy" . . . "what they did is bad.": Carol Milstone, "When Bad Kids Think They're Great," *National Post* (Canada), March 23, 1999.

173 Researchers Kasser and Ryan . . . children who do the same : T. Kasser, R. M.Ryan, M. Zax, and A. J. Sameroff, "The relations of maternal and social environments to late adolescents' materialistic and prosocial values," *Developmental Psychology* 31, no. 6 (1995): 907–14.

176 Neurophysiologist Wolfram Shultz . . . off of their own: Jason Zeig, "Brain Tour: It's a Pleasure," http://money.cnn.com/2002/09/16/pf/investing/agenda_brain5/, September 27, 2002.

177 According to Piaget: Christopher Peterson and Martin E. P. Seligman, *Character Virtues and Strengths* (New York: Oxford University Press, 2004).

178 "each more adequate at responding to moral dilemmas than its predecessor.": Lawrence Kohlberg, "The Claim to Moral Adequacy of a Highest Stage of Moral Judgment," *Journal of Philosophy* 70, no. 18 (1973): 630–46, jstor.org/stable/2025030.

179 Psychologist Carol Gilligan argued . . . in his research): Carol Gilligan, "In a Different Voice: Women's Conceptions of Self and Morality," *Harvard Educational Review* 47, no. 4 (1977).

179 Kohlberg further built on Piaget's . . . throughout one's life.: Lawrence Kohlberg, "The Development of Modes of Thinking and Choices in Years 10 to 16," Ph.D. dissertation, University of Chicago , 1958. and W.C. Crain, *Theories of Development* (Prentice Hall, 1985), 118–36

179 psychologist Erik Erikson . . . character and virtues: Christopher

Peterson and Martin E. P. Seligman, *Character Virtues and Strengths* (New York: Oxford University Press, 2004).

181 created the following chart . . . Erikson's eight stages and the resulting character development. Strengths of Wisdom and Knowledge Chart: Christopher Peterson and Martin Seligman, *Character Strengths and Virtues* (New York: Oxford University Press, 2004), 60–2.

183–184 As Matt Davidson, president and director of education . . . "unique character strengths *and* weaknesses": excellenceandethics .org/blog/author/matt-d/ –January 28, 2011.

184 "Failure syndrome" . . . from unearned self-esteem: Carol S. Dweck, *Mindset* (New York: Random House, 2006).

185 Sonja Lyubomirsky has discovered the benefit . . . The impact on well-being is far greater: Sonja Lyubomirsky, *The How of Happiness* (New York: Penguin Press, 2008), 128.

185 In *Character Matters*, Thomas Lickona recommends that the child ask . . . reported on the front page of my hometown paper: Thomas Lickona, *Why Character Matters* (New York: Touchstone, 2004), 47.

188 "coaches must provide accurate praise . . . virtuous behavior": R. Ginsburg, S. Durant, and A. Baltzell, *Whose Game Is It Anyway?* (Houghton Mifflin, 2006), 5.

CHAPTER 9. GETTING YOUR STORY STRAIGHT ABOUT ACHIEVEMENT

193 "Talents are best nurtured in solitude. Character is best formed in the stormy billows of the world."—Goethe: inspirational -quotes.info/character.html.

196 Sir Edmund Hillary . . . "under a rock to die": http://neveryet-melted.com/categories/mark-inglis/.

197 "The weakest of all weak things . . . in the fire": Mark Twain, "The Man That Corrupted Hadleyburg," *Harper's Monthly*, December 1899.

197 "Things that appear . . . the long haul": Daniel Coyle, *The Talent Code* (New York: Bantam, 2009), 18.

198 "Positivity transforms us for the better . . . new ways of being": Barbara Fredrickson, *Positivity* (New York: Crown, 2009), 24.

198 In his book *Man's Search for Meaning* . . . achievement and growth: Viktor E. Frankl, *Man's Search for Meaning* (Boston: Beacon Press, 1959).

199 "The test of a well-functioning conscience . . . given lip service for the sake of appearance": Polly Young-Eisendrath, *The Self-Esteem Trap* (New York: Little, Brown, 2008), 83–84.

209 "Am I doing the right thing with my life? . . . Am I happy?": William Deresiewicz, "Solitude and Leadership," *American Scholar* (Spring 2010), http://www.theamericanscholar.org/solitude-and-leadership/.

CHAPTER 10. WINNING WITH YOUR NEW SCORECARD

211 "There are two things to aim at in life . . . the wisest of mankind has achieved the second."—Logan Pearsall Smith: brainyquote.com/quotes/quotes/l/loganpsmi105541.html.

213 "The scoreboard said I lost today . . . take you and the memory of you with me for the rest of my life": Andre Agassi, *Open* (New York: Knopf, 2009), 378.

216 WSJ article regarding Sign on a hospital door . . . "The Management": "Let's Be Worthy of Their Sacrifice, 'The wounds I received I got in a job I love,'" Karl Rove opinion piece, *Wall Street Journal* Online, January 2, 2009, http://online.wsj.com/article/SB123085828475347775.html.

218 "Your life is happening right now . . . your life will be full": Chris Ballard, "The Courage of Jill Costello," *Sports Illustrated,* November 29, 2010, 70.

INDEX